150+ Ways

to Win Over Customers
and Make That Sale

*The Tested and Proven Techniques &
Strategies that Clinch the Deal*

150+ Ways
to Win Over Customers
and Make That Sale

Christopher Hopkins

PNEUMA SPRINGS PUBLISHING UK

First Published 2008
Published by Pneuma Springs Publishing

150+ Ways to Win Over Customers and Make That Sale
Copyright © 2008   Christopher Hopkins
ISBN: 978-1-905809-36-3

Cover design, editing and typesetting by:
Pneuma Springs Publishing

A Subsidiary of Pneuma Springs Ltd.
7 Groveherst Road, Dartford Kent, DA1 5JD.
E: admin@pneumasprings.co.uk
W: www.pneumasprings.co.uk

A catalogue record for this book is available from the British Library.

Published in the United Kingdom. All rights reserved under International Copyright Law. Contents and/or cover may not be reproduced in whole or in part without the express written consent of the publisher.

Best Wishes
Chris Hopkins
Oct '08

This book is dedicated to my mum Phyllis, who has devoted her life to her husband, children and family.

Contents

INTRODUCTION 11

SECTION I 13

1 HOW TO GET PEOPLE TO TAKE ACTION 14
Focus On The Problem 14
Your Solution To The Problem 15
Establish Your Credibility 15
Get Your Prospect To Act 16

2 LONG SALES LETTER OR SHORT? 17

3 KEEP YOUR WRITING SIMPLE 20

4 HOW TO WIN OVER YOUR READERS 22
Gaining Trust 23
Remind Them About Their Problem 23
The Importance Of The Postscript 24
Hold Your Reader's Attention 24

5 THE ONE IRRESISTIBLE STATEMENT THAT'S ALWAYS SUCCESSFUL 26

6 HOW DO YOU WRITE A WEB SITE THAT SELLS? 28
How To Write An Irresistible Headline 29

7 HOW TO MAKE YOUR WRITING MORE APPEALING 35
Bullets 35
Keep Your Paragraphs And Sentences Short 36
Adapt Your Writing Style 36
What Is Your Principle Selling Position (PSP)? 38

8 THE KEY FEATURES TO A SUCCESSFUL WEB SITE 39
Choose Your Content Carefully 39

Tell Your Visitors All About You 40

9 HOW TO WRITE EFFECTIVE LONG COPY 41
When To Use Short Copy 41

10 HOW TO CREATE AMAZING HEADLINES
AND SUB-HEADLINES 43
Powerful Words 44
Create An "End Result" Headline 45
Solve A Problem 45
The Solution To The Problem 46
List The Benefits 47
Offer Free Bonuses 48
Offer A Firm Guarantee 48
Ask For The Order 49
Generate A Sense Of Urgency 50
Include A P.S. 51

11 KEEP YOUR COPY SIMPLE 54

12 GRAB YOUR READER'S ATTENTION 58

SECTION II 63
HOW TO START-UP AND RUN A SUCCESSFUL
ON-LINE SALES BUSINESS 64

13 HOW DO I BECOME A PROFESSIONAL
         SALESPERSON? 65
What To Sell 65

14 SELF BELIEF 67
Don't Be Afraid Of Failure 68

15 FINDING CUSTOMERS 69
How Do I Get Customers To Buy My Product? 69
Be Enthusiastic 70

16 HAVE CONFIDENCE IN YOUR ABILITY 72
17 ASK QUESTIONS 75
How Do Needs Start? 75

18 FEATURES AND BENEFITS 78
Closing 79

19 THERE'S ALWAYS ROOM FOR IMPROVEMENT .. 82
Attention To Detail 83

20 HAVE THE RIGHT ATTITUDE 84
Have Clear Goals 86
Make Know Your Strengths And Weaknesses 86
You Must Things Happen 87

21 TRUST 89
Testimonials 91

22 SUCCESS DOESN'T COME EASY 93

23 WHAT MOTIVATES A CUSTOMER TO BUY? 96
Do That Little Bit More 98
Create A Good Impression. 98
Use Your Time Wisely 100
Coping With Rejection 101
Trustworthiness 102
Persuasion 103
Product Knowledge 104

24 HONESTY 105

25 PRICE 107

26 CUSTOMER REQUIREMENTS 110

27 TAKE IT SERIOUSLY 112
Prioritise Your Tasks 112
Do The Important Jobs First 114
Know Your Product 116
One Step At A Time 117
Time Management 119

28 CUSTOMER SATISFACTION 122
Try To Do More 124
Find Your Niche Market 126

29 STANDARDS OF EXCELLENCE 128

Be Optimistic 129
Choose The Right Product 130
Why Do People Buy?... 130

30 ESTABLISH YOUR INTEGRITY 133
Customer Relationships... 134
Never Leave The Customer Feeling Manipulated 136
Believe In Your Product... 136

31 THE POWER OF PERSISTENCE............................. 138

INTRODUCTION

The biggest obstacle to success that faces on-line businesses is lack of traffic. If nobody visits your website, you're not going to generate enough sales to make your business grow and develop. You've got to attract visitors to your site if you want to be successful.

Fortunately, there are lots of ways to make your site more appealing. Because more people are choosing to use the internet to do their shopping, far-sighted businessmen are thinking-up ingenious ways of attracting visitors to their sites.

This book will show you the basic methods of establishing a powerful marketing technique that will drive increasing amounts of traffic to your website. Isn't this what every business wants?

You are about to learn the proven methods on how to entice customers and make them eager to know more about what you're offering. Using these techniques will ensure that your prospect is riveted to your message and therefore more inclined to do what you ask, (buy from you).

You'll learn how to get people into the right state of mind where they become so interested in your website that almost nothing else matters. And, if you follow my instructions you'll also get your readers to take action.

Section I

Chapter 1

HOW TO GET PEOPLE TO TAKE ACTION

There are two ways to motivate people to take action. That is either through pain or pleasure. Most experts in marketing conclude that the first motivator (pain) is more effective than the second (pleasure).

Put simply, this is how it works:
1. Open with a statement that will get the prospect's full attention.
2. Focus on the problem that the prospect has.
3. Offer a solution to the problem.
4. Let the prospect know how much better off he will be once he has purchased your product or service.

Focus On The Problem
When it comes to writing your headline you should begin by drawing your prospect's attention to his immediate problem. Let's say you sell a cure for acne, your headline should begin:

> Suffer from acne?

Likewise, if you're selling an anti-wrinkle product, you could say:

> Want to look younger?

What you're doing is attracting people by focusing on their problem.

As you're probably aware by now, the question you're asking is "What problem does my visitor have?" And once you've found out what the problem is, you can create a lead headline that addresses it.

So, your first task is to get your readers attention by focusing on his problem.

Your Solution To The Problem
Secondly, after getting your reader's attention, you then refer him to your solution. In the case of the "acne" headline, the follow-on might read:

> New cream gives you completely clear skin in 30 days

Or the anti-wrinkle ad might say:

> My revolutionary approach has changed the lives of Thousands of people just like you....
> I can help you too.

As you can see, what you're doing here is showing how you can solve the problem that you unearthed at the beginning of your headline.

This will keep your prospect interested because you are totally focusing on his problem.

Establish Your Credibility
Next, you need to make people believe in both you and your product or service. Customers are naturally sceptical; they've probably been sold poor and shoddy goods in the past, and

are therefore reluctant to part with their money unless they are sure that what you say is true. They are on the defensive because they've seen unbelievable and unsubstantiated claims on other websites; so they want to be certain that you can deliver. Therefore, you need to think of ways to convince them that you are trustworthy.

You could do this by stating:

> Your acne will disappear in 30 days or I will refund all your money

Or

> Studies have shown that wrinkles significantly decrease after only a few applications

Get Your Prospect To Act

Lastly, you must get your prospect to take action and purchase your product or service. People want to be guided and told exactly what to do. They won't do this unless you spell it out for them. Therefore, you must take them by the hand and tell them how to order your product and how much it will cost them to do so.

For example:

> Order my acne cream today...... You'll be glad you did Tomorrow.

Or

> Order my revolutionary anti-wrinkle cream today for only $9.99.

Remember, the method for persuading people to buy is:
1. Make a powerful statement in order to get their attention.
2. Remind the prospect about the problem he is experiencing.
3. Let the prospect know how he will benefit from buying your product or service.

Chapter 2

LONG SALESLETTER OR SHORT?

People will read any amount of words on a website provided they are relevant to their needs. Therefore, you need to make sure that you grab your readers attention and keep hold of it. If you do, you will be on the road to success, guaranteed.

The general consensus amongst professional copywriters is:

YOU WILL SELL MORE, IF YOU TELL MORE

What this means is it's probably best to use long copy (lots of words). It's the perceived wisdom that sites with long copy tend to be more successful. But bear in mind, they must be attention grabbing words. I'm sure I don't have to tell you that as soon as a visitor to your site gets bored they will leave, never to return again.

The length of copy on your website should depend upon the price you're asking. The more money you're asking for, the longer copy you should use. (Remember: copy means words).

You must use as many words as are necessary to describe your product or service in detail.

Your main priority must always be to focus on the needs of the people who visit your web site. They are perfectly happy to read long copy, provided it is interesting and relevant to their situation. If you find that people aren't staying on your web site, this means you haven't addressed their needs or interests.

One way to make sure you're doing it right is to methodically list all the sensible reasons why people should buy your product; and also the reasons why they may choose not to. Every one of these should be mentioned in the copy.

Once you have listed the benefits, and dealt with the possible objections, you should have the ideal content to persuade people to buy.

In order to get an enquiry, you need to list the benefits of your product or service. If you do this successfully it should substantially reduce the number of objections.

The other important ingredient needed for an effective copy is an appealing, attention grabbing opening. It is essential that you edit over and over again to eliminate unnecessary words; otherwise, as I stated earlier, your prospect will become bored and leave your site. Also, make sure you list things in the right order; benefits must be listed before features. (I will be going into greater detail about the difference between features and benefits later on in this book).

An important fact to remember is that advertisements with more than 1000 words are read significantly more than those with fewer words. Even most people in advertising are unaware of this statistic.

You must also write from your reader's perspective, not your own. Try to understand what they are looking for. When you understand what your reader wants you will then be able to write something that will appeal directly to him. If you don't grab his attention immediately I don't have to tell you again what'll happen do I? You know from your own experience that when you browse through a magazine you only read the articles that are of interest to you. You don't read every single article, do you? You just flip through the pages until you come across something that you find interesting. Well, it's exactly the same for people who are browsing through your web site. They will only be looking for things that interest them.

Understand that your reader only cares about himself. So you have to give him what he wants; not what you want. See things from his perspective, and from his perspective only. The easiest way to do this

is to imagine that your reader is a selfish child who care about nothing and nobody, except himself. If you try to see things from the reader's point of view, you'll be better equipped to write something that will totally hold his attention and have his eyes glued to the page.

Chapter 3

KEEP YOUR WRITING SIMPLE

When writing your sales letter, there's no need to use big, complicated words; rather, just let the dialogue flow. Pretend you're talking to a friend or relative. You wouldn't talk to a friend in a way that would be difficult for him to understand, would you? Well, it's exactly the same when writing your web site, you should keep it simple. Try to write in an undemanding and direct style. Simply say what you have to say in a way that anybody can understand. A simple trick is to pretend you're writing for a child. If you do this, you'll write in a manner that absolutely everybody will find easy to comprehend.

Bear in mind, if your reader doesn't understand what you're saying, then you haven't succeeded in writing in a way that clearly conveys your message.

Most people wrongly believe that writing must be intellectual. They couldn't be more wrong! Always keep your writing simple. Instead of using a long word, try to find a shorter one. As I said earlier, pretend you're talking to someone close. So, if you wouldn't use the word in everyday conversation, don't use it in your writing.

Pretend you're writing your article for just one person. This is a good way to develop a closer relationship with your readers. It's worth bearing in mind that even though thousands of people will read your web site, each one is an individual. So, write your sales letter as if it was intended for just one person, in the style of a letter, and you will create a personal rapport between you and your readers.

Be conscious of the fact that everybody is busy and pressed for time,

so make your writing interesting and exciting. Don't use over-long sentences or complicated statements. Keep your writing clear and concise and avoid any unnecessary words, sentences or phrases. If you do this, you'll be writing in a way that everybody finds interesting.

Chapter 4

HOW TO WIN OVER YOUR READERS

The bottom line is, if you want to be successful in business you must be able to win people over and get them to act. But how do you motivate them? What does it take to do this?

When writing your web site, your main aim is to get people's attention so they can fully understand what you're telling them. One way to ensure that your reader is gripped by your words is to create a sensational headline that they will find impossible to ignore.

Another approach is to highlight their needs. For example, if you're selling slimming aids, the main concern of the people who need this service is to lose weight. See, it's obvious, isn't it? So, your attention grabbing headline might say:

> A Revolutionary New Kind of Weight Loss Programme

Or

> The Most Advanced Weight Loss Programme Available

Tell your readers how you can solve their problems and you'll have them well and truly hooked.

You must ask yourself, "What is my reader concerned about?" You must ensure you thoroughly address these concerns in your sales letter. Remember, you must convince him that your product or service is the solution to his problems.

Alternately, your headline could ask a question that leads the reader over to your way of thinking. This headline might say:

"If there were a way for you to lose weight easily, would you want It?"

As you can see, your reader can only answer this question with a "yes!" This is because you're offering him what he needs and wants.

Gaining Trust

To gain your reader's trust it is a good idea to obtain testimonials from people who have used your product or service and were happy with the results. Simply ask these people to supply you with a short written statement stating what they think about your product or service and how it improved their situation. If they are too busy, or simply don't want to write one, you can write it for them and ask them to sign it. (I will go into greater detail about testimonials later in this book).

Another sure way to gain the trust of your reader is to offer a firm guarantee. The sad truth is, if you don't have some kind of guarantee, hardly anyone will have enough trust or confidence in you to buy what you're selling.

Remind Them About Their Problem

Don't end your sales letter without reminding your readers about their specific problem and, even more importantly, that you have the solution to this problem.

The Importance Of The Postscript

I cannot stress strongly enough how important it is to include a P.S. Reader's are naturally drawn towards a postscript. It's what most people (including myself) read first.

Your P.S. is your opportunity to state the main benefits your readers will gain by purchasing your product or service. To tell them how it will transform their lives. That the price of your product or service is a small amount when they consider that it will repay itself many times over. Paint a picture that people can see as they read your words.

Use your P.S. to tell your reader about your guarantee or to offer free gifts as an incentive. People like free gifts; it gives them the sense that they're getting something for nothing. It also makes them more susceptible to what you're offering.

It's best to make your strongest points in your P.S. Tell people how your product is guaranteed to please and how it will satisfy all their needs.

Remember, the P.S. is the section that most people go to first and the part that makes the greatest impression.

Hold Your Reader's Attention

Try to make your writing pleasing to the eye. Use short paragraphs with wide margins. It's also advisable to alter their length, otherwise your writing becomes too predictable. When people are browsing through web sites they are more likely to stay on the ones that have short, crisp paragraphs, rather than ones that ramble on and on.

If people like the look of your web site they will be far more likely to read it. A useful tip is to stagger your right-hand margin, and not have a solid block of text. This makes it far more easy to read. First impressions are crucial when it comes to attracting prospects.

Readers are also drawn towards quotation marks. Whenever

quotes are inserted into a section of text people tend to read that section before any other. This is because people are always eager to find out what other people have to say about almost anything. It's just human nature, we're all naturally inquisitive. So, whenever you feel it is appropriate, satisfy your reader's curiosity by quoting what somebody else said.

Chapter 5

THE ONE IRRESISTIBLE STATEMENT THAT'S ALWAYS SUCCESSFUL

If you overwhelm your prospect with numerous reasons why he should buy your product or service you run the risk of boring or even annoying them. Your writing can become bland and stale rather than exciting and stimulating. But, if you give him one irresistible statement he will feel compelled to do whatever you request.

If you can grab your reader with that ONE enticing statement, you will have him hooked. The reason being that you have offered him the one tempting benefit that he really wants and needs.

There are those who believe that you have to bombard people with reasons why they should buy your product or service; also that you must have a stack of testimonials as proof of its quality and reliability. This approach works in many cases, but if they only knew how much their sales would improve with the inclusion of one tantalising statement, it would blow their minds. If that one irresistible statement is delivered correctly, they might not even need the other long list of reasons to buy.

But, to ensure you hit the target with that statement you must know what your prospect wants and needs. Once you have established this, you will be in a position to cater to these desires with a strong statement that really packs a punch.

So, say you're selling shampoo, you could list the many benefits and features, such as: "pleasant fragrance", or "guaranteed to get rid of dandruff". These statements contain information that the prospect will find useful; but neither of them are guaranteed to have the major impact that is needed to make your product seem irresistible. You must conjure up a statement that is so powerful it will totally captivate your reader and convert him from someone who is slightly curious about your offer into someone who must have what you're selling.

This means that if your prospect suffers from dandruff, the one thing he wants is a shampoo that will rid him of it. So, in this case you must put all your effort into coming up with a strong statement that says how your shampoo is: "Everything you've ever wanted from a dandruff shampoo" or "Guaranteed to totally eliminate dandruff within days" or maybe "The perfect solution to the problem of dandruff". In each instance you've come up with a one-line statement that says exactly what the prospect wants to hear; namely that your product will get rid of his dandruff. Period. Anything else you add will probably seem timid by comparison and may even irritate him. This is because by informing him that you have the solution to his problem, you have already told him the only thing he wants to hear.

The best way to write an irresistible statement is to do it exactly the same way as you would write a headline. This means you should make it short, appealing and applicable to the needs of your prospects. In other words, think about what your prospect wants and needs; then present him with one solid statement that says you can give it to him. Remember to keep your statement short, captivating and dynamic.

After all, it only takes one good line to persuade someone to buy.

Chapter 6

HOW DO YOU WRITE A WEB SITE THAT SELLS?

What is obvious about the title of this chapter?

Have you spotted it yet?

It's not too difficult is it?

The answer is, I asked you a question. Didn't you spot that? In fact, I've already asked you four questions in this chapter, haven't I? (that's five).

Questions are a phenomenal way to attract people and hold their attention. The reason being that when you use a question in your first line, people are compelled to read the next line. They want to find out the answer to the question. That's why you carried on reading this, isn't it? (six).

So, the answer to the question I posed in the title of this chapter is "Ask Questions". But the questions must be open-ended if you want to capture the imagination of your reader.

If the question you pose can be answered with a simple yes or no there's no incentive for your prospect to keep reading. You'll have no bait to dangle in front of him and he'll quickly lose interest; and you'll lose a potential customer.

But, by asking an open-ended question such as: "How Do You Write a Website That Sells?" it is impossible to answer this question without reading the rest of this chapter.

So, using the technique of asking open-ended questions is an extremely effective way of keeping visitors glued to your web site.

How To Write An Irresistible Headline

Your headline is the most important part of your sales letter as it is the very first thing your visitors see. It's the key to determining whether or not your web site will be successful in grabbing people's attention and exciting enough to make them want to read-on.

But, there's another essential ingredient needed to lure visitors further into your sales letter, this is the sub-headline. Sub-headlines assist in getting your message across and keeping people curious and enthusiastic about what you're offering. You may need to create a considerable amount of sub-headlines in order to convey your message; so don't worry about using too many, you'll soon discover that they are all necessary.

Writing a strong web site is both a science and an art. To be successful at it you must stick to the fundamental rules of copywriting. If you do you should produce a written promotion that will sell your product or service. But, bear in mind it is the writer's imaginative and inventive flair that makes the writing distinctive and special.

When you are so comfortable with these basic rules that they become second nature, you'll be able to move forward into a new, more successful, worthwhile and productive type of writing. This section is aimed at getting you to that level of writing.

The headline is what draws in the reader and keeps him gripped for long enough to read the entire sales letter.

The headline is always in bold type and lures the visitor with a compelling question or statement. It's quite normal to spend more time preparing and writing the headline than you spend on the entire sales letter. That's how important it is to make sure you get it right.

A headline must immediately capture the reader's attention and keep him glued to the screen. Once you've succeeded in doing this, instructions, facts and benefits can be brought into play.

Successful headlines are short, snappy and easy to read. They can be any of the following:

A Compelling Question:
Looking for that special something?
Tired of the same old ....?
Who could say no to ....?
Isn't it about time you ....?
What's the best investment you could make?
Could you use an extra $.......... each month?

Brash Statements:
A once-in-a lifetime opportunity.
Now you can earn more than you ever dreamed of.
You'll wonder how you ever managed without it.
Discover why our customers keep coming back for more.
Nobody else comes close.
There's simply no comparison.
Be the success you were meant to be.
You've dreamed about it, now you can do it.

Guarantees Of Value:
Get more for your money.
Gives you so much for so little.

Unbeatable value.
Eminently affordable.
Savings Galore.
So much for so little.
Save time and money.
Worth its weight in gold.

How-to:
How to get where you want to go.
How to unlock the power of your subconscious mind.
How to write and publish your own novel.
How to successfully sell your product.

Here are some other ways to create a perfect headline:

<u>Open With These Words</u>
Announcing!
At last!
Hurry!
Unique Opportunity!
Last Chance!

<u>Target Your Specific Market</u>
Housewives!
Builders!
Weight watchers!
Embarrassing Acne!
Sore Back!

<u>Show The Benefits Your Product Can Offer</u>
Learn to write a winning ad in 10 days!
Free from embarrassing foot odour in 10 minutes!

Overcome your phobias with my revolutionary New Method!

Discover the Secret to Making Easy Money.

Offer A Free Gift
=================

Buy one, get one free.

You'll also receive a ………….. at no extra charge.

Included at no extra cost.

Free gift!

Free book on Internet Marketing.

Include Testimonials
====================

"XYZ know how to treat their customer" (Joe Smith).

"XYZ cater to all your needs" (Bill Brown).

"XYZ gives you professional, courteous and personal attention" (Sam Green).

"Other companies may offer the same deal as XYZ, but not the same service" (Jed Black).

"XYZ impressed me in a way I'll never forget" (Ralph White).

The inclusion of a testimonial enhances your credibility enormously. The reader's eyes are naturally drawn towards quotation marks. But you must always use genuine testimonials from real customers, and get their permission each time. As I stated earlier, people want to know what others think; they can be won over by the opinions of others. Therefore, if the person supplying the testimonial is someone with similar interests to your prospect, this is bound to influence his decision. Reinforcing your message with testimonials adds an element of trustworthiness to both you and your product.

Use The Words These And Why
These boots are fully waterproof.
These pills are easy to swallow.
Why our customers always come back.
Why our product is so popular.
Why these hats are the height of fashion.
Why these techniques really work.

Make It Seem Easy
Easy way to achieve success.
Easy way to lose 30 pounds in 30 days.
Easy way to remove stubborn stains.
Easy way to restore old furniture.
Easy way to write a book.
Easy way to build confidence.

Emphasize The Benefits
This helpful book will show you the main strategies for taking charge of your life.
These simple exercises will help you tap into your hidden strengths.
This simple programme will teach you skills you'll use your whole life long.
These natural ointments will bring out the natural beauty of your skin.
This scientifically tested formula is designed to tackle even the dirtiest jobs.

By stressing the benefits of your product or service you're showing your prospect how it will improve his life. But you should always write with his best interests in mind. Once you switch from self-centred writing to customer centred writing, you'll be on the right track.

Reveal A Positive Outcome

Softer, smoother skin in a matter of days.
Healthier gums in 10 days.
Leaner, shapelier legs in 14 days.
Increases energy levels day after day.
Watch your money grow month after month.
You'll be writing creative copy in no time.

Tell Them Why

Three reasons why you should use these creams.
Four reasons why you should read this book.
Five reasons why you should use these techniques.

By giving reasons you are answering the age-old question "What can you do for me now?" This is what the customer needs to know before he will consider entering into a business relationship with you. By satisfying his needs you will be creating an emotional bond with him. It may bring to the surface basic needs he has, such as to feel secure, organized, healthy or successful. Therefore, if your writing connects with your reader, it should motivate him into action; and action from your reader is exactly what you want, isn't it?

The bottom line is, you want your reader to be curious and eager to know more about what you're offering. But to have this effect on him, your writing must hit the target.

Chapter 7

HOW TO MAKE YOUR WRITING MORE APPEALING

Anyone is capable of creating compelling, effective and high quality sales copy, regardless of their level of education. As long as you stick to the principles outlined in this book, you can have a web site that is powerful and successful.

In this chapter I will show you various ways to make your web site much more appealing to your visitor.

Bullets

One way of making sure that your visitor doesn't get bored and leave your web site is to use bullets(.). These serve as a welcome distraction to your visitor, who can often become wary of reading page after page of nothing but a solid block of text. Bullets are an effective way of emphasizing the benefits of your product or service.

A bullet is a dot, star or asterisk. They can be used anywhere in your text, and they never fail to get results. The reader's eye is naturally drawn to a short list of bulleted points. They deliver your message quickly and effectively. Keep the list to a reasonable size, as listing too many points will only serve to lessen their impact.

- You'll see the results in less than 24 hours.

- Designed to tackle even the toughest jobs.
- These proven techniques will put you way ahead of the field.
- Easily assembled and ready to use.
- The perfect business companion.
- Effective, efficient, and economical.
- Style, comfort, and refinement.
- Safe, strong, and versatile.
- Superior value with professional results.
- Gives you the competitive edge you need to succeed.
- Guaranteed for a lifetime.

Keep Your Paragraphs And Sentences Short
Paragraphs that are short, crisp and direct are extremely powerful. So, whenever possible, keep them short and to the point. Remove any unnecessary words or phrases, and don't use pretentious language. A useful rule of thumb is to pretend you're writing for a child. Use simple language to say what you want to say using the words you'd use if you were talking to a friend.

Short, powerful words give your writing an intensity and character all of its own. The prospect finds it far easier to read, and is therefore less inclined to click onto another site. People are basically lazy, they won't stay long on a site that's full of long, incomprehensible words or technical jargon. You must always write in a way that grabs people's attention and keeps them glued to the screen. Short, sharp paragraphs and sentences achieve this every time.

Adapt Your Writing Style
You may have to alter your writing style in order to be in tune with the people you're targeting. Use a style that flows

smoothly and that's clear, concise, engaging and persuasive. Avoid long, complicated sentences; instead adapt a firm, but warm and genial tone. You must do everything you can to make sure your web site is inviting and appealing, otherwise it won't get read.

Construct your sentences and paragraphs in a style that compels people to read your writing. You must also write in a way that subtly manoeuvres people around to your way of thinking, and coaxes them into taking the actions you want.

Keep your writing fresh and exciting. How you achieve this is up to you. But you must always ensure that you grab your reader's attention and keep hold of it.

Here's an example of how you can re-arrange a sentence to make it more appealing.

You might have a line on your web site that states:

> "My product is very popular"

You could change this to:

> "As you read more and more of this web site you'll be convinced that my product is bound to become a market leader and be in demand for years to come."

Notice the difference?

The first quote is dull and unimaginative. But the second quote is exhilarating and rousing. It contains an instruction and a deduction. When these two are incorporated they compel the reader to take action.

But, if you want to create compelling copy (writing), you must focus entirely on the needs of your readers, not your own. With this in mind, now is probably a good time to look over your web site and delete anything that isn't relevant to the interest of your readers. This may mean having to completely rewrite entire paragraphs, add applicable phrases, or do whatever is necessary to keep your visitors attention fully focused on your site.

What Is Your Principal Selling Position (PSP)

The principal selling position is your product's or service's most appealing benefit in the eyes of your prospect. The PSP should be the focal point of your copy (from this point onwards I shall be referring to writing as copy). In order to decide which of your product's many benefits will be your PSP, you must look for the one which will have the greatest impact on your targeted audience.

When you have decided upon which of your product's benefits will be the most advantageous to your prospect, you have singled-out your PSP.

Chapter 8

THE KEY FEATURES TO A SUCCESSFUL WEB SITE

Your web site must serve your visitors needs in a way that's simple and easy to understand. It's no good investing all your time, effort and cash in order to attract more visitors, only to have them desert you because they can't find what they're looking for. You must make it as easy as possible for them to find their way around your site.

Make those first vital seconds count and grab your visitor's attention immediately, otherwise he will leave your site and never return. To successfully do this you have to make sure that the first page of your web site grabs hold of your visitor's attention by introducing an irresistible benefit that tempts him to stay longer in order to find out more.

Choose Your Content Carefully

Before you design your web site, you must know what it will contain. This is standard practice, all experts do it. Designers and architects use written plans and blueprints to help them visualize the end result. In the same way, you too must plan and develop your copy with a structure that captivates your reader's imagination and motivates him to such an extent that he feels he must have what you're offering. Some proven techniques include strong headlines, benefit-oriented copy, and a bulleted list of key points.

Tell Your Visitors All About You
People like to know who they're dealing with. Informing visitors about your company and yourself helps to create trust. It's vitally important that the customer has complete faith in your honesty and integrity. If he doesn't, it's highly unlikely that he will want to buy anything from you.

Include a photo of yourself, and tell people exactly what your web site is all about.

Another way to establish your credibility is by providing your visitors with contact information. This should not only include your e-mail address, but also your mailing address and telephone number.

It's important to bear in mind that, regardless of what kind of web site you have, it's vitally important that you gather as many of your visitors' e-mail addresses as possible before they leave your site. It would be naïve to assume that every visitor to your site is going to buy from you on their very first visit, so it's essential that you make a note of their names and e-mail addresses for future reference (promotions, newsletters, special offers etc.). But, in order to obtain your visitors e-mail address, you must give them a valid reason to let you have it in the first place.

As I have already informed you, many first time visitors to your web site will leave without buying anything. So, it is imperative that you request their names and e-mail addresses as quickly as possible. If you leave this until they reach the second page of your site, you'll run the risk of losing possible contributors who haven't read that far.

Make sure you get your visitor's Christian names, surnames and e-mail addresses. This will enable you to send them personalized e-mails later on.

Chapter 9

HOW TO WRITE EFFECTIVE LONG COPY

You must have powerful sales copy on your web site in order to convince potential customers about the benefits of your product or service.

Many people think that a few sentences of copy is sufficient to turn their visitors into purchasing customers; they couldn't be more wrong. What's needed is a thoroughly detailed sales copy that guides your visitor through all the necessary steps of the sales process.

Long copy sales letters tend to be between 8 to 10 pages long, but they can also be as long as 20 or 25 pages. These carefully planned letters are intended to lead the visitor through a proven sales procedure.

You should seriously consider using long copy if:

- You are selling one product, or one type of product (i.e. 10 styles of waterproof coat, all giving exactly the same benefit).
- You are selling a service.

When To Use Short Copy

Given that long copy is so effective, why would anyone ever consider using short copy? Well, in certain situations it makes more sense to use short copy. For instance, long copy won't work if your site is in the style of a catalogue, introducing your company's whole product line with complete descriptions. In this instance copy should be kept brief and informative. Products should be arranged into categories, price ranges, or any other appropriate system.

It's usually a good idea to show similar or connected products together on a single page or spread; you're more likely to get numerous purchases by doing this.

Don't write page after page about each and every product, you'll never reach the end. Also, it will thoroughly bore your visitors. This doesn't mean that catalogue style sites do not need sales copy. Even if a long sales letter isn't appropriate for your web site, you must still find a way to guide your visitors through precisely the same sales process that's needed for a long sales letter.

Chapter 10

HOW TO CREATE AMAZING HEADLINES AND SUB-HEADLINES

The headline and sub-headline are the all-important sections of your sales letter. They are the first things your visitors see when they click onto your web site. Therefore they should be gripping, compelling and powerful enough to hold their interest and tempt them into reading more of your sales letter.

A winning headline can have a colossal impact on your sales, so it's worthwhile spending a considerable amount of time on getting it just right. It must be crammed with benefits that are relevant to your readers needs and be tempting enough to have them desperate to discover more.

Provided your headline and sub-headline are powerful enough to grab hold of your reader's attention, you should now be able to steer him onto your opening paragraph. This is where you lure him still further by reminding him about the problem he has; the problem that made him visit your site in the first place. He probably clicked onto your site hoping that your product or service would be the solution to his problem; your job is to convince him that it is.

If possible, use your headline to demonstrate your USP (unique selling proposition). To achieve this you must show your visitors how your product is superior to a similar product being offered by your competitors. Therefore your headline should contain answers to questions like:

- Does my product cost less than my competitors?
- Is my product more reliable than my competitors?
- Does my product have more features than my competitors?

In other words, what makes your product or service unique?

Powerful Words

Your headline must contain powerful words that pull your readers in and leave them eager to find out even more. There are certain words that are guaranteed to make people sit up and take notice.

Whenever possible, try to include powerful words like these in your headlines:

- **Free!**
- **Exclusive Offer**
- **Save**
- **Attention**
- **Introducing**
- **Announcing ……**
- **Prices slashed!**
- **Win ………**
- **Only**
- **Unlimited**
- **Absolutely**

- **Urgent**
- **Important**
- **Last chance!**
- **New!**
- **Bargain**
- **Great news!**
- **Sale**
- **Successful**
- **I**
- **We**
- **Proven**

- Amazing
- Hurry
- Guarantee
- Nothing
- At last

- Enjoy
- Results
- Easy
- Don't miss
- Breakthrough

Create An "End Result" Headline

Powerful headlines are usually ones that guarantee an end result. People are attracted to headlines that promise a benefit to them. For instance:

"How to get ...."

"Discover the secrets of ...."

"Learn the easy way to ...."

"How to increase your ...."

"How to reduce your ...."

"How to" headlines are extremely effective. This is because people crave information; they're simply drawn to "how to" headlines that not only give them a benefit, but also solve a problem they have.

Solve A Problem

Your customers need to know what problem your product or service can solve. Provided your headline and sub-headline generated enough interest in your readers, they should be curious enough to read on into your opening paragraph. This is where you remind them about the problem they're probably experiencing; a problem that your product or service can solve. But a problem that will continue unless they buy your product or service.

Tell your reader why he needs your product or service, but without giving too much information away at this time. This way you will leave him increasingly curious and excited about your product; so curious that he will feel compelled to find out more.

After establishing your credibility through the use of testimonials (I will deal with testimonials in greater detail later on in this book) you need to prove to the prospect that you are the solution to his problems.

You achieve this by making clear to him why you are in a position to offer a solution to his problem, then support this claim by providing testimonials from satisfied customers. Whilst it is important to establish your credibility at the outset, you must be careful that you don't dwell on this for too long; otherwise your prospect will become bored and stop reading. Rather, give him sufficient cause to trust you enough to read on further.

The Solution To The Problem
Once you've made the reader aware of his problem and gotten him to the point where he trusts you, it's now time to introduce your product or service as the solution to his problem. There's no need to go into any great detail at this stage, just restate that you're guaranteeing him a solution to his problem.

As I explained earlier, bulleted points are a powerful way of stressing your product's principal benefits. They're easy to read and the reader's attention is naturally drawn towards them. The list should contain examples of your product's foremost benefits plus important facts.

List The Benefits

By listing the benefits and features of your product or service you are able to show the reader how you can solve his problem. The best way to achieve this is to link a powerful benefit to every feature. The difference between a benefit and a feature is:

> **Benefits:** show your prospect what your product or service can do for them. How it will make them happier, richer, or free from anxiety and stress.
>
> **Features:** simply focuses on the qualities of your product or service.

As an example, below is a list of product features coupled with the benefits that can be gained from these features:

Product Feature	Benefit To Customer
Lower in calories	Makes you look slimmer and healthier
High return on your investment	Helps you to live more comfortably
Costs pennies a day to operate	You save money!

So, draw the reader's attention to the benefits your product or service offers, and how these benefits will solve their problems. Instead of trying to sell people your product, you should be trying to help them. Using this approach, you are far more likely to get sales. A good way of highlighting your benefits is to have a bulleted list of attractive and compelling points that will grab your reader's attention.

Don't worry about piling too many benefits into your sales

copy. If your list contains appealing, irresistible benefits, you can never have too many. If you want to convince your readers about the value of your product or service, a list of bulleted points is the best way to achieve this.

Offer Free Bonuses

Even though your readers may be convinced that your product or service will be the solution to their problems; and although they are satisfied that you are reliable and trustworthy, they may still be reluctant to hand over their money. If this is the case, by including free bonus items, you will prove to them that they're getting far greater value for their money. People always like getting something for nothing, it's human nature. So, by offering free bonus items at no extra charge, you'll actually stir your readers into taking action. They really do have a dramatic effect on your sales and, as is the case with benefits, you can never have too many free bonus items.

Offer A Firm Guarantee

It's important to have a firm guarantee in your sales letter, otherwise you'll experience difficulty in closing sales. In many cases, the inclusion of a guarantee is all that is needed to persuade an unsure prospect to go ahead and purchase what you're offering. A firm, strong guarantee helps to lessen any concerns he may have about buying from you.

Contrary to popular belief, the longer your guarantee is good for, the less returns you're likely to receive. You may find this hard to swallow, but it's actually true. If you offer a lifetime guarantee on your product or service you will receive fewer returns than if you offered a one-year guarantee. You'll also get fewer returns if you offer a one-year guarantee than you will for a thirty day guarantee. The reasons for this are:

- People feel more assured that what you're offering will

be as good and dependable as you described it to be. A long guarantee indicates to them that you have absolute faith in what you're selling.

- The customer doesn't feel under any pressure to rush to a judgement for fear of over-running the thirty day return period. Instead, he knows he can take his time in deciding whether or not your product or service satisfies his specific needs.

A solid guarantee can dramatically alter the way the customer perceives you. It shows him you're trustworthy and reliable. But, best of all it gives him the peace of mind of knowing that, if he isn't satisfied, you'll give him back his money. It's extremely important that you gain the trust of your customer; especially on the internet, where the majority of your first-time prospects won't know anything about you and therefore won't be sure if they can rely on you to deliver on your promises.

If a customer is undecided about whether or not a product is worth buying, do you think a twenty day guarantee will persuade him to buy? The answer is no! Whereas a full year's guarantee stands a far greater chance, and is far more likely to get you that sale.

Ask For The Order
Unless you can persuade the customer to take action you run the risk of letting him off the hook and losing him before you've had a chance to close the sale. You must invite him to take action with a powerful statement that compels him to buy. It's really that simple, but you'd be surprised at the amount who overlook this. You must forcefully and boldly ask for the order.

Now that you've offered your prospect your guarantees and bonuses, he should no longer be apprehensive about spending his money. This means he is ready to make the purchase. He just needs you to tell him what to do. I cannot stress strongly enough just how hugely important this is to your future success. If you neglect to ask for the order at the right point you will definitely lose a vast amount of business. The customer will probably read your sales letter to the end, but because he's been given no guidance on how to order, he'll simply drift onto another site.

Therefore, it's vital that you boldly ask your potential customer for the order, and show him exactly what to do. It's probably a good idea at this stage to remind the customer about his original problem and re-state how your product or service is the ideal solution to this problem.

So, tell your readers exactly what to do, and ensure that your instruction are concise, definite and thorough. Remember, without clear instructions, all the work you put into creating your sales letter will be squandered.

Here are a few examples of the kind of instructions you should give to your readers that show them exactly what they should do next:

- Write, fax or e-mail for further information.
- Call today to take advantage of this limited offer.
- Order your .... today while stocks last.

Always ensure that your close gives the customer sufficient information on how to proceed with the sale once he has accepted your offer.

Generate A Sense Of Urgency
By this stage your reader is likely to be on the verge of making a buying decision. It's at this point that you must introduce a sense of urgency, otherwise he may decide to think about your offer and make a decision later. The danger with this is that sometimes people forget to come back or,

even worse, decide they want to take up your offer but can't remember how they found your web site in the first place, and are therefore unable to return to it.

So, by instilling a sense of urgency, you're able to pressurize your readers into making an immediate decision. You can instill a sense of urgency in the following ways:

- If your offer is available for a limited period of time "Available for the next seven days ONLY!"
- Restrict the number of products or services you're able to offer.
"Available only to the first 100 people who order!"
- Include discounts or bonus items on a limited amount of products for a limited amount of time.

As I stated earlier, if your readers don't have a good reason to purchase immediately they may decide to put it off till later, then you run the risk of them forgetting all about it.

Include a P.S.
It's important to include a P.S. in your sales letter, equally important as requesting the sale. Many visitors to your site will simply flick through it quickly, picking-up the occasional word here and there; but if you include a P.S. they tend to read these more thoroughly. This is because their eyes are naturally drawn to them. But, in order to get this response you must pack your P.S. with benefits, solutions to problems, urgency, and requests for the order.

Use the P.S. to remind your prospect about your offer, restate some major benefits he will obtain; and stress yet again that he must take action immediately, otherwise he won't be eligible to receive your product at the specially reduced price, nor will he receive the special bonus offers.

You must also let the prospect know what will happen if he

doesn't take action right away; how much time and money he will waste, and how much more stress and inconvenience he will experience. You then restate that by ordering now he won't have to endure these problems any longer, because your product or service is the ideal solution to them.

It's worth noting that when people receive letters they almost always turn to the end to see who it's from. This is why so many professional salespeople use a P.S. in their sales letters. Research has shown that the majority of readers remember the P.S. more than any other part of the letter.

Remember, the P.S. should contain important facts; it should also re-emphasize your offer and stress the need for urgency.

Here are some examples:

> "These .... are disappearing fast. So please send us your order today."

> "Don't forget, you must reply by 10th July to be eligible for this special offer."

> "Remember, if you wish to enter this competition, you must do so before 20th September. You're under no obligation to buy anything: simply return your entry form."

> "To claim your free ...., simply use the enclosed reply form to send us your order today.

You must use the P.S. to:

- Ask for the order
- Generate a sense of urgency
- Highlight the benefits of your product or service.
- Draw attention to your no-risk guarantee

The P.S. can be so influential that it's worth considering using more than one in your sales letter. You might think this is a bit excessive; but bear in mind that the P.S. can contain an absolute wealth of information.

Chapter 11

KEEP YOUR COPY SIMPLE

The way you layout your sales letter is just as important as the way you write it. But you must always remember the most important rule: "Keep It Simple!" Basically this means that it should be easy for your prospects to read. If you clutter your web site with unnecessary bolding and colours or too many capitals you will only succeed in making it more difficult for your reader to understand your sales copy.

To make your copy easy to read you must:

- Avoid spreading your text over the entire width of the screen as this makes it far harder to read. An ideal width is 500 or 600 pixels.

- Don't centre large amounts of text; only centre a small number of major benefits and key points. Keep your right margin staggered because a solid block of text is not appealing, and it's far more difficult to read.

- Use the same two or three font styles and sizes throughout your web site, otherwise it will appear cluttered and over-elaborate. This also applies to headlines and pop-ups.

- Try not to over-use bolding, colours and italics, or they'll eventually lose their impact.

- Don't use graphics and images just for the sake of it.

Ensure that every image used is necessary and connected to what you're offering, i.e. pictures of your product or service. A photo of yourself is usually helpful too.

- Don't be tempted into using elaborate backgrounds. They only serve to make your text more difficult to read. A simple white background with black text is always a winning combination.

Your sales letter should be set-out something like this:

HEADLINE
Containing heaps of attractive and irresistible benefits to tempt your visitors!

SUB-HEADLINE
Highlight the benefits of reading this sales letter and instil a sense of urgency that makes your visitor think "I must read this now!"

FROM:
(your name)

Dear Reader:
INTRODUCTION: Draw the reader's attention to the problem that your product or service will solve.

BODY: Prove your credibility, reliability and honesty.

BODY: Identify with your reader and his problem.

BODY: Tell your reader how your product or

service will solve his problem and outline what it does.

BODY: Use bulleted points to describe the benefits of your product or service.

> Outline major benefits
> - Point No.1 - Summarize how the reader will benefit from owning your product or service, and explain why.
> - Point No.2 - State a second benefit and once again explain why.
> - Point No.3 - State a third benefit etc. etc.
> - (list further benefits).

BODY: Tell the reader how much your product costs and why it's this price. Then explain why this is a reasonable price.

CLOSE: Include heaps of bonuses and your reader will feel he is getting greater value for his money. Make him think that he'll miss out on something amazing if he doesn't order now. This should compel him to take action.

CLOSE: Always ensure that you include a firm guarantee. This completely removes the element of risk and allows the customer to purchase without feeling anxious or concerned.

CLOSE: Ask for the order! Plainly and firmly tell your reader how to purchase your offer.

REGARDS:
(your name)
(your position within the company - if applicable)

P.S. Include a powerful postscript to remind the reader about the benefits of owning your product or service, and to instil a sense of even greater urgency.

_____

Chapter 12

GRAB YOUR READER'S ATTENTION

Writing a convincing and compelling copy is both a science and an art. To be successful at it you must follow the basic guidelines that I have shown you, then you'll be able to create a persuasive copy that will sell your product or service.

Like other professions have tools of their trade, your tools are the words you use to lure your readers. The most effective words are the ones that sell. Powerful adjectives like:

Sensational	Captivating
Sumptuous	Breathtaking
Exhilarating	Remarkable
Tantalizing	Stunning
Spectacular	Exclusive
Unforgettable	Irresistible

And timeless phrases, such as:

You can depend on ……..	Remarkable results
Guaranteed to ………	Unmatched performance

Sheer bliss

Experience the wonder of ……..

No-risk offer

Irresistibly priced

Success guaranteed

High performance

Look no further

Packs a punch

Or

Gives you instant access to ……..

At the flick of a switch

Wherever and whenever

At your convenience

For any occasion

Built for efficiency

Guaranteed for a lifetime

Satisfaction guaranteed

Risk-free - satisfaction guaranteed

All you need for the job

So very versatile

For professional results

Within easy reach

Flexible design

In a flash

Fast acting

Works immediately

Ready to use

Mad to last a lifetime

A recipe for success

Prompt service

Personal attention

At the touch of your fingertips

Easy to use

And, of course, the old favourite:

FREE!

Remember, you only have a matter of seconds to capture your reader's attention. In that time you must do everything in your power to turn him from a reluctant sceptic into someone who is eager to buy your product or service. By using the right words in the right way you can alter the way your reader views both you and your product, even to the extent where he feels compelled to make a decision to buy.

A successful website is one that sends a powerful message about both you and your product or service. It entices readers with information they can use and also motivate them to buy from you. Web copy should be sharp, lively and concise if it is to succeed in holding the attention of an impatient audience. On your home page especially, use brief but tempting statements to encourage your readers to click on each link. Use sub-headings to break up your copy, but not too many or your page will look cluttered. Give your web site a character all of it's own, one that stands out in the crowd.

Writing a winning web site means writing a web site that sells. Every feature of your site should play a part in bringing you to your ultimate objective; persuading your visitor to buy your product or service.

The first fold of your site is the most important because this is where your visitor decides whether he wants to stay or go; and remember, it only takes him a matter of seconds to make up his mind. This is why your headline needs to be so powerful and persuasive. Never underestimate the importance of your headline. Get it wrong and you've lost both the customer and the sale; get it right and your success is virtually guaranteed.

The sales copy is the most important aspect of the entire sales process, so you must always ensure that it is powerful and compelling. It must engage the emotions and appeal to the reader's curiosity. Use a natural, uncomplicated writing style that follows everyday speech patterns.

Constantly revise and edit your work. Delete everything that doesn't serve your writing. Cut out all the dead wood. Trimming your writing will help to tighten it and strengthen your material. This may mean having to delete entire sections or write entire new ones, but sometimes this is what's needed to get the best results. Look at your web site with a critical eye and delete or rewrite the parts that you think people would skip past. Every word should pull its weight.

To write effective copy you use words as your tools to persuade and motivate your readers. You convince them that you have something valuable to offer and you compel them to acquire it for themselves.

The techniques I've taught you will enable you to turn words into power; and then use this power to make whatever you're selling seem irresistible to your reader.

Section II

HOW TO START-UP AND RUN A SUCCESSFUL SALES BUSINESS

This section is designed to help you gain the skill and confidence needed to start-up a successful sales business working from home. Making money from home is now far easier than it ever has been. The arrival of the internet has made communication quicker, simpler and cheaper. Earning money from home not only helps meet household bills, but it also gives you a purpose in life, helping to avoid sinking into the pit of frustration, boredom or even depression, which can so easily happen if you don't keep your mind active.

I know get rich schemes are common; usually in newsagents windows, unsolicited junk mail or spam e-mail. I don't promise to make you an overnight millionaire - I would never make that claim. The amount of money you make will depend upon your enthusiasm and attitude. But, if you follow my advice you will become a professional salesperson and a winner.

Chapter 13

HOW DO I BECOME A PROFESSIONAL SALESPERSON?

A common misconception is that salespeople need to have a well-rehearsed sales spiel or script. This is wrong, customers can see right through this and it automatically creates suspicion. Sales spiel is not a part of professional selling.

Most people actually enjoy buying! They like being sold to professionally. That is the essence of the professional seller. You must create an atmosphere that is pleasurable for your buyer.

Also, product knowledge is extremely important, but enthusiasm is by far the most essential asset when it comes to selling.

What To Sell?

Finding a product that suits your need is a delicate balance of weighing-up both the pros and cons. What skills and expertise have your acquired over the years and how much time space and money can you put into your business.

If you are unsure what product you want to sell it would be helpful to make a list of the advantages and disadvantages of each product you consider; because you must realize that a project undertaken without proper planning can become a financial burden, rather than a source of income. But, if you plan properly, this is very unlikely to occur.

A week spent planning your future is time well spent. Get to know your product, because as a salesperson you must be credible. You must be able to convince your customer that what you are selling is what they really need.

A good starting point in making money from home can be your current job, or a profession you have been involved with in the past. There are a great many advantages in doing similar work, the most important being: you already have knowledge in this field, and have presumably already made the necessary contacts. This can only be to your advantage, as it will give both you and your customers confidence; which in turn will help you build a positive attitude, all of which are essential if you are to be successful.

You should also be aware of your competitors' products, prices and main selling points. This information is readily available on the internet.

Remember, if you do not have product knowledge, you will be unable to exert any real pressure on your prospective customer to buy.

There will be times when you are caught out by a question. In these instances it is quite acceptable to apologize to the client and tell him that you will get back to him as soon as you have the answer. But this should be the exception, not the rule.

Draw up a list of your targets and set a time frame for achieving them. People always try to meet deadlines; but be realistic, don't set your goals too high.

SUCCESSFUL PEOPLE ARE METICULOUS PLANNERS - THEY LEAVE VERY LITTLE TO CHANCE

Chapter 14

SELF BELIEF

If you don't believe in yourself, nobody else will! You must build a positive frame of mind.

Never fall into the trap of saying "I can't", this is incredibly self-destructive. Once you start thinking negatively, you begin to lose your self-belief, which is a vital part of your business armoury.

Avoid negative thoughts, they are dangerous, destructive and corrosive. Instead say to yourself "I can" and "I will". It's amazing the effects that these two statement can have. They can completely alter your state of mind; you begin to think more positively and imaginatively, and discover that you actually can.

You must remember that although you are at a disadvantage when competing with large businesses, you do have one enormous asset on your side: you are an individual. Large organizations won't be able to give their customers the "personal service" that you can; and if you treat your customers well, they will recommend you to people they know, and before you know it, you have built-up a reputation as a company that is a pleasure to do business with. So bear in mind, bigger isn't always better.

By setting yourself realistic targets and planning meticulously to meet these targets, you will be giving yourself a chance to believe in yourself.

You must develop the right attitude, you can do anything you really desire. Your ability hasn't anything to do with it; it's how much you want to succeed that counts. Everyone has the ability to improve. You can, and will if you really want to.

Have confidence in your ability; this comes from familiarity. It's when we try something new that we feel a lack of confidence.

Don't let yourself get into the habit of making excuses for under-performance. Never say "it's not my fault". If you are in business alone, who else's fault could it possibly be?

Don't Be Afraid Of Failure

People are conditioned into believing that failure is the most terrible thing that can happen to them. You must learn to stop thinking this way. Instead, you must develop the habit of thinking that every failure brings you a little bit closer to success. Look upon each failure as a minor setback that you can learn lessons from. Almost every successful person has had many failures along the way, but they persevered until success finally came.

Remember, you haven't failed at anything until you actually give up.

When things are going well in business, life is great. It's when business isn't doing quite so well that the positive person must remain optimistic and draw on all his or her resources to get back on track.

So, remember to always think positively and constantly say to yourself "I can" and "I will".

AVOID NEGATIVE THOUGHTS LIKE THE PLAGUE

Always think of yourself as a winner, and remember: failure can never triumph over persistence.

Chapter 15

FINDING CUSTOMERS

Changes in market trends means that, however successful you are, or however good your product or service is, your business is bound to feel the effects. Products become outdated, businesses that were once regular customers can fold or move into different areas. It's at times like these that you, as a professional salesperson must get new business. You must have a system for finding new customers.

Your first port of call at times like this should be past customers. It's far easier to sell to somebody who has previously done business with you. You have already built-up a relationship, and they will know you to be trustworthy and reliable.

How Do I Get Customers To Buy My Product?
There's only one way to get somebody to do something, and that's by making them want to do it. When you show a person what they want, they'll go to extraordinary lengths to get it. The most important rule in salesmanship is to establish what the customer wants, and then help him get it.

There are basically two driving forces that motivate people to take action, and they are: the desire for gain, and the fear of loss.

Try to see things from the buyer's point of view. Think in terms of his wants, needs and desires.

In your advertising literature and on your website, don't use the personal pronoun "I", or "we". Instead use "you" or "your". Also, ask questions in your literature. One of the best ways to get a customer to buy is to ask pertinent questions; it helps to crystallize their thinking.

This usually results in the customer convincing himself that he needs your product or service.

Asking questions is a very effective way of getting the customer to think positively about you and your product. This is vitally important, because if the customer doesn't have faith in you or what you are offering, he will look elsewhere.

You must have faith in your product. If you don't, nobody else will. But you must never make exaggerated claims about it's benefits. Instead you should cultivate the habit of understatement.

To be a successful salesperson you must have confidence in your ability, this will win you the confidence of others. Learn all there is to know about your product or service, and keep learning.

TAKE TIME TO THINK AND PLAN AHEAD

It's amazing how much you can get done when you take the time to plan ahead; and it's equally amazing how little you get done when you don't.

Be Enthusiastic

Train yourself to act enthusiastically and you will become enthusiastic.

Enthusiasm is contagious. If your customers see how enthusiastic you are about what you are selling, chances are they'll be more eager to go for it. They will be carried along by your positive attitude.

Nobody is a natural salesman. You've got to mould yourself into whatever you want to be, but you must be prepared to put all your effort into achieving this goal. One of the greatest pleasures in life is knowing you have done something to the best of your ability.

If you're having difficulty in organizing yourself, set aside one day each week to prioritize your tasks into areas of importance. Proper planning leads to a more organized and stress-free life.

Ask questions. Questions, instead of positive statements can be the most successful way of getting the sale, or guiding customers to think along similar lines to you. It's a more subtle way of selling.

Gain the confidence of your buyer. You should not ask if the customer believes in your product, but rather "DO I BELIEVE IN MY PRODUCT".

Chapter 16

HAVE CONFIDENCE IN YOUR ABILITY

To have confidence in yourself, and gain the confidence of others, you must know you business inside-out, and strive to know even more.

People admire a salesman who is honest and sincere. The customer must completely trust you; if he doesn't, it is unlikely that the sale will go ahead.

If you indicate to a person that you want to sell him something that will cost him money, you are as good as saying that you want to increase his problems. But if you are able to convince him that your product will solve a vital problem of his, he will be far more receptive.

The first, and probably the most important rule in selling is "FIRST OF ALL, SELL YOURSELF!"

Only after you have gained the trust of your customer, can you begin selling your product or service.

New customers are probably your best source of new business. Assuming they have been treated well by you, they will be happy and proud of their recent purchase. They will probably feel excited and enthusiastic and will be eager to tell their family, friends and acquaintances about it.

Always take time to ensure that you have fully served your

customer's best interests. That way he will remember you and choose you over your competitors when he comes to making further purchases.

IF YOU LOOK AFTER YOUR CUSTOMERS, THEY'LL LOOK AFTER YOU

The four stages in a typical sale are: Attention, Interest, Desire and The Close.

If you want to be successful in selling, you've got to get the basics so firmly in your mind, that it almost becomes part of you.

Eliminate the fear of failure. Failure is a weakness which is common to most people. If you learn to conquer your fear of failure, success will come eventually. That's guaranteed.

Just keep going! Failure cannot triumph over persistence.

You have to be passionate about what you do. They say that if your passionate about what you do, you never do a day's work in your life.

Successful salespeople rarely know what makes them so successful. They often do things naturally without ever realizing what they are doing differently to the average person. The best way to learn what makes these people successful is to observe them in action, and not to make the mistake of asking them to describe their skills. This way you will observe that: Successful salespeople have discovered that virtually every sale involves finding things out by asking pertinent questions. Asking questions helps to establish your customer's needs and get a better understanding of his situation.

You will have to show your customer that you have a useful product that will solve his problems. In every sale you must convince the customer that you have something worthwhile to offer.

Lastly, you must obtain some kind of commitment from the customer to purchase your product or service.

Chapter 17

ASK QUESTIONS

The basic truth is, you can never persuade a person about anything. But, if you ask the right questions, you can guide the customer to persuade himself. All successful negotiators use questions, as opposed to reasons to persuade their customers to buy their product.

Customers buy because of their needs. These needs are uncovered through questions. But it's important that you ask the right kind of questions. The right questions will guide your customer to the conclusion that your product or service does solve their existing problems or meets their specific needs.

Let's first establish exactly what a need is. A need can be defined as:

Any concern expressed by the customer which you, as the seller, are able to satisfy.

How Do Needs Start?
The first sign that we have a need is when we no longer feel completely satisfied with our existing situation. We begin to feel discontented about how things are, and realize that there is definitely room for improvement. So, feelings of

dissatisfaction and discontentment are usually the first signs of a genuine need.

Once dissatisfaction begins, it gradually begins to grow. We soon begin to perceive other problems and difficulties that may arise. At this point, it becomes a great deal easier for somebody to persuade us to buy their product, especially if they can persuade us that it will solve our problems and improve our present situation.

But this isn't always the case. In some instances, the perception of a problem, no matter how big, doesn't automatically suggest that we're ready to purchase. You must transform this need into a commitment to act by turning the customer's needs into desires or intentions to buy.

You should ask the customer questions pertaining to his problems; these will uncover his present difficulties, dissatisfactions and needs. Problem questions are an essential ingredient in successful selling.

The more problem questions you ask, the greater are the chances of you making a successful sale. Problem questions have a very positive effect on customers. Once you satisfactorily prove that your product or service can solve a customer's problem, you're potentially providing him with something useful.

PROBLEMS AND NEEDS ARE WHAT MOTIVATE PEOPLE TO BUY

If you want to be successful in selling, all you have to do is get more orders, but how do you do that? One way, as I've already shown, is to find out your customer's needs, and then offer him a solution to them. Another way is to demonstrate to the customer the desirability of owning your product or service, and how it will enhance his life.

These two methods - one which uncovered the problem, and the other which focused on the solution are both highly successful, and will guarantee that you obtain more orders.

But remember, you must convince the customer of the seriousness of his problem before you can even begin to demonstrate the desirability of your solution.

The main purpose of asking questions is that it convinces the customer that, what he perceives as a small problem, is actually a large enough problem for him to take immediate action. Sometimes it is necessary to demonstrate to the customer that the problem is bigger than he thought.

Another advantage that comes from asking pertinent questions is that they can build up the value of the solution which your product offers. They also focus the customer's mind on the solution instead of the problem. The customer begins to foresee the benefits of your product. These questions have a positive effect on the customer and are extremely successful in building good customer relations.

Only the customer can have a full understanding of his problems and needs. Pertinent questions focus their minds on the solution you propose; and they are usually more likely to buy if they feel it was their idea to solve their problem by purchasing your product or service.

So, once the buyer has surmised that his problem is big enough to warrant taking action, you should then focus his attention on the benefits of your product, and how it would be the solution to his problems.

Questions are so simple, and yet they can be so advantageous to the seller. Clever questioning can have a very positive effect on the customer; it can build up your customer's enthusiasm to the point where he is eager to make a purchase.

Chapter 18

FEATURES AND BENEFITS

Features and benefits are the two ways in which you describe your product or service.

Features are merely facts about the product, but benefits actually show how the features can be beneficial to the customer. Features don't really help you to sell, but they don't hinder you in any way either.

In contrast, benefits are extremely helpful in a number of ways, such as:

> They describe how the features can help the customer.
>
> They demonstrate what your product offers them, and what your competitors products don't, or can't.
>
> They motivate the customer to buy.
>
> They demonstrate how they can fulfil the customer's needs.

To put it simply, benefits are more appealing than features. Benefits entail demonstrating how you can fulfil a need which the customer has. Customers are more likely to buy from you when you can give them what they want.

Customers are more likely to have concerns about the price of your product if it contains a lot of features. This is because the customer expects to have to pay a higher price for products with more features.

But, if you can sell your product for a cheaper price than your competitors, in spite of all the extra features, the customers concerns will subside and he will feel more positive.

If customers have doubts about the value of what you're offering, it's probably because you're not developing their needs sufficiently. If they do feel that your product is too expensive, this tells you that you haven't built up their needs to a point where they feel they should buy. The solution to this is to concentrate less on the features, and instead, focus on asking problem questions.

Experts say that if you can tap into an area of personal interest to the customer, then you're guaranteed to form a good relationship, which is essential to your success.

Over the years customers attitudes have changed. Years ago customers would say that they bought from a certain person because they liked him. But nowadays they're more likely to say that they like a certain person, but they prefer to buy from his competitors because they're cheaper. So, it seems that customer loyalty is a thing of the past.

Closing

Closing is anything that induces the customer into making some kind of commitment to buy.

No other aspect of selling is as popular as closing. It is unquestionably the most important of all the selling techniques; yet it is probably the hardest to master. If it's done wrongly or clumsily you can lose more business than you gain.

Closing is a method of applying pressure to the customer in order to induce him into making a decision. You will usually find that with a small buying decision, the pressure tends to yield positive results. But this is not the case with larger decisions. People tend to react negatively to pressure in bigger buying decisions.

So, we can conclude that: the bigger the buying decision, the less effective closing techniques are likely to be.

The general rule is that pressure is more likely to be effective when applied in small buying decisions than in larger ones.

Price also determines whether or not you will be able to close the sale. The lower the price of your product or service, the more likely are the chances of your closing techniques being successful. But, the higher the price the less likely they are to be so.

Never underestimate your customer. They are probably more intelligent and sophisticated than you give them credit for. They will quickly see through sales spiel. So, you could find that a closing technique which would work on a less aware customer might be totally ineffective on a more sophisticated one. So, don't assume that all customers are gullible enough to be persuaded and enticed into buying by closing techniques.

By using closing techniques, sellers apply pressure on customers in order to get a decision from them. Customers are less happy about decisions they feel they've been pressurized into making; rather than ones they've made of their own free will. For this reason, you should be extremely cautious about using closing techniques, especially if you intend doing further business with this customer.

To summarize, in low-cost sales with unsophisticated customers that you don't have need of a future customer relationship, closing techniques can be very effective. But, if you want to sell on a larger scale, where you will be dealing with more intelligent and sophisticated buyers, with whom you wish to form a lasting business relationship; closing techniques will be less successful, and can even hinder your chances of getting the sale.

So, don't put too much emphasis on closing; but equally important, don't totally disregard closing altogether. There is also evidence which shows that the omission of a closing technique can damage the sale.

It seems that, regardless of all the disadvantages of closing techniques, if you fail to employ any closing whatsoever, you are unlikely to be successful in obtaining commitment from your customer. But how do you obtain commitment without using closing techniques? Doing nothing isn't an option. The sale won't close itself.

Chapter 19

THERE'S ALWAYS ROOM FOR IMPROVEMENT

As we've seen earlier, as a result of asking pertinent questions you can get the customer to realize that he has an urgent need to buy. Closing techniques aren't required when the customer already wants to buy. So, you have obtained a commitment without the need for any closing techniques. Because you convinced the customer through the use of clever questioning that he needs what you're offering, he has closed the sale for you.

Just reading this book won't improve your selling skills. There's no quick and easy way to learn any skill. The only way you can guarantee success in anything is through practice. You must be willing to invest a large amount of time to turn the knowledge you've learned from this book into practice.

To successfully learn a new skill, it's best not to overstretch yourself at the start. Begin by picking one new behaviour to practice. But be sure you've completely mastered this new skill before you even contemplate moving onto the next one. Remember, the first time you try anything new, it's bound to feel awkward and uncomfortable. But don't be put off by this; if you persevere it will take you to a higher level, and that can only be good news. If you keep practising, you will eventually feel comfortable using these new skills.

You have to practice any new behaviour many times before you feel totally comfortable using it. But, once you get over the initial stage, you will become extremely effective and successful.

Attention To Detail

See your product or service as a solution to your customer's problems. Don't think about your product only in terms of it's features and benefits, but also in terms of the problems it is able to solve.

It is attention to detail which will, above all else, ensure your success. Successful salespeople attach great importance to constantly reviewing their performance; they're continually looking for ways to improve. They never see themselves as the completely finished article. They also recognize that their success depends upon attention to detail. They know their products and services inside-out; and are constantly striving to learn even more, so as to have the edge over their competitors.

So, never sit back and think your job is done. There is always room for improvement; search hard enough and you'll find it. This is the attitude you must adopt if you are to become a successful salesperson.

Chapter 20

HAVE THE RIGHT ATTITUDE

Top salespeople are confident, optimistic, positive and self-assured; they have both their business and personal life under total control. A positive attitude and an optimistic attitude towards yourself and your work is essential if you are to grow. This, together with total self- confidence is what is needed if you are to achieve your goals in life.

So, to be successful in selling you must set yourself higher goals, and know how you are going to achieve them. You should draw-up a detailed step-by-step plan of what you need to do to achieve what you desire Remember, you're in charge. If you don't like what's going on in your business, then you should change it for the better, and do it right now.

If you see yourself and your product or service as problem solvers, this attitude will be picked-up by the customer; and he will view you and your company in a more positive way. Instead of viewing you as mere vendors of goods; or someone who just wants his money, he will see you as a dedicated professional who has the solution to his problems. Therefore you should focus your attention on understanding the customer's situation, so that you will know what the customer actually needs.

As I mentioned previously, you must become an expert in

your field and know your product inside-out. You must also familiarize yourself with every single detail of your product or service: including it's features and benefits, and it's advantages and disadvantages. If your customers feel that you have good product knowledge, it gives them greater confidence in you, and it can give you the edge over your competitors.

To be a top salesperson you should set yourself clear targets for what you want to achieve, and then work out meticulously how to see this through to completion. Think carefully about what you must do, and when you have made up your mind, act decisively.

Once you have a clear plan of what you must achieve for success in sales, you will feel far more relaxed and confident. You will definitely know which direction you are headed in; the direction that leads to success and happiness.

You must set high standards for yourself, and always strive to meet these standards or, better still, surpass them. You should be extremely ambitious, and always believe you are capable of greater things. You will be surprised at the effect that this positive thinking can have on your sales performance.

You must also care about your customer, and ensure that you work with honesty and integrity. Your primary job should be to guide your customer into making a good buying decision. If you treat your customer the way you would want to be treated if you were in their position, they will be more likely to do business with you in the future.

A positive mental attitude is essential if you are to be successful in any business venture. There are bound to be some setbacks and disappointment along the way; but you should remain strong, resilient and optimistic, in order to bounce back from these inevitable occurrences. A positive mental attitude is the characteristic of a winner, and this is what will ensure your success in selling.

For you to achieve success in sales, you must be prepared to work hard and diligently for a long period of time; this could be months, or perhaps even years. This is essential if you want to earn the kind of money that you desire. To be successful in any type of business, you must be prepared to invest a great deal of you time and effort into it, over a long period of time.

YOU WILL ONLY GET OUT OF YOUR BUSINESS WHAT YOU PUT INTO IT - NO MORE OR NO LESS

You must decide where you want your business to be a few years from now, and how you are going to get from where you are now to where you want be in the future. When you are sure about where you are coming from and where you want to get to, you become far more effective at realistically planning for the future. You should have a goal to increase your sales by a certain percentage (say between 10 and 20 percent each year), and plan the best way to achieve this.

Know Your Strengths And Weaknesses

Good salespeople are those who know their own strengths and weaknesses and who therefore tend to concentrate their efforts into dealing with the type of customers that are more likely to buy from them.

You should also be aware of what talents and skills you bring to your business. Will these skills and talents be beneficial to your company? Will they increase your sales? And what areas of your business do you need to improve upon?

You Must Have Clear Goals

Clear and written goals focus your attention and concentrate your mind on the direction you intend to go, and what you want to achieve. With clear, specific goals you will accomplish a great deal more than you otherwise would have, and you will have greater vision and clarity. But the greatest benefit to goals is that they give you far more confidence and enable you to feel far more in control of events. This is because you are absolutely clear about what you want to achieve.

Thinking carefully and planning thoroughly will greatly increase the likelihood of you reaching your targets. Your success depends upon thinking through both your personal life and your business in advance; and then creating a detailed plan of how you are going to get where you want to go.

When you start working slowly and methodically towards something of great importance to yourself, you find yourself developing a strength and persistence that helps you achieve things that you wouldn't have previously thought possible.

Make Things Happen
Successful salespeople carefully position themselves so as to gain the maximum advantage in the marketplace. They always make good use of their time so as to achieve the best possible results. They are never satisfied with their present situation, and always aspire to something greater. They never wait for things to happen; they go out and make them happen.

Your aim in life should be to fulfil your full potential and be fully committed to becoming a top salesperson. Try to become everything that you're capable of becoming; both in business and in life in general.

When you advertise your business you should be able to confidently state why the customer should choose your company over your competitors; and what he will gain by making this choice, that he otherwise wouldn't have.

We all have the capability to become experts in our chosen field. By knowing your strengths as a salesperson; and then working on improving those strengths, you too can become a winner.

Chapter 21

TRUST

Trust is the foundation upon which successful and long term business relationships are built. If your customer knows he can place his trust in you, he will often buy from you without even enquiring about the price.

If you are seen as a person of honesty and integrity, you will find yourself getting a lot of business through "word of mouth". People will recommend your business to their friends and relatives simply because you have shown that you care about your customer.

Top salespeople understand that their success depends upon the relationship they develop with their customers, and they don't allow anything to jeopardize this.

Some customers will be reluctant to enter into a long-term relationship with any seller. This is usually because they have purchased products in the past that they wish they hadn't, and they therefore view salespeople as untrustworthy and unreliable.

Building trust is essential for your success. Once you have established this, it is essential that you maintain it. The level of trust that the customer has in you is the vital component that starts the whole sales process. When you focus all your attention on your customer's needs, he instinctively begins to trust you more.

People don't like to think that they are being pressured or manipulated into buying goods; rather they prefer to feel that they've been assisted into making an intelligent buying decision.

When the customer makes a buying decision, he is relying on you to honour the promises you've made. You break these promises at your own peril; the consequences can be catastrophic. The worst thing that can happen to any business is to develop the reputation of being untrustworthy or unreliable.

The establishment of trust is essential as it alleviates the customer's concerns about risk; which is one of the biggest obstacles to getting the sale. If you establish trust at the outset, it can have a positive impact on sales in the months and years that follow.

Customers prefer to stick with their existing seller rather than go through the upheaval of switching to someone new. So, once you've obtained a regular customer who has confidence in you, the chances are he will remain with you.

Your aim should be to develop long-term relationships with your customers rather than going for a quick single sale, where you don't anticipate ever having to deal with them again. This is not the way to run a successful business.

Remember, the more you show that you care about your customer, the more likely it is that they will want to do business with you in the future. Also, the more positive you are about your company and services, the more confident the customer will be in you.

Credibility is an absolute necessity if you are to be a successful salesperson. It is taken into consideration during every transaction that relies on you. The customer must know that he can depend upon you to fulfil your promises; he must believe you will do what you say you will do.

Testimonials

A good way to achieve credibility is to include testimonials from satisfied customers on your website or sales literature. You will find that they are such a powerful addition that they can often be the overriding factor when it comes to making the sale; they can be the difference between success and failure. It gives the prospective buyer far more confidence in you and your product if he sees that others have bought it and are happy with it. If you don't have any testimonial letters, then I would suggest that you try to obtain some as soon as possible. If you've been in business for any length of time, you should have some favoured customers who will only be to happy to write a testimonial letter for you if you ask them.

Obviously, if you're just starting-up in business this will not apply to you. But, once you begin to obtain regular customers, I strongly recommend that you take this course of action.

A list of your satisfied customers is another way of proving your credibility.

An impressive testimonial is an extremely strong weapon to add to your armoury. Make a conscious effort to collect as many of them as you can. Once you start incorporating testimonials in your sales literature and on your website, you will find that, almost overnight, your sales will dramatically improve.

You increase your credibility by proving to the customer that your product or service has the precise benefits that he is looking for. If you can prove that what you are selling is perfect in every way for the customer, this will increase the chances of making the sale.

You should be constantly looking for ways to show how your product will actually save the customer money in the long run. If you can convince him that the product will actually pay for itself in the long-term, he will be far more inclined to buy.

If you can back up your claims about your product or service with guarantees offering total cash refunds if the customer is not completely satisfied, this will give both you and your product enormous credibility. This is a very powerful tool that builds your customer's confidence in you and your product; the confidence that is essential to get the sale.

It is essential in business today that you continually build and maintain good quality relationships with your customers. Once you acquire a customer, you should make every effort to keep hold of him indefinitely. You originally create customers by convincing them that your offering the best value goods, and that you are reliable and care about your customers.

You must, once you have obtained these customers, do everything in your power to hold onto them. The best way to do this is to deliver on your promises, meet or exceed their expectations and continue to build upon your relationship.

You should always be completely honest and trustworthy, and treat the customer in the way you would want to be treated. Always ensure that you help the customer to make the right buying decision; the one that is in his best interests. The customer must be completely confident that he has made the right decision in buying from you, and that he will have no regrets in choosing you over your competitors.

Chapter 22

SUCCESS DOESN'T COME EASY

To be successful in business takes a lot of hard work, and selling is no exception to this. If you think that selling is going to be an easy route to making easy money, you are in for a terrible shock. People who believe this usually end up totally demoralized when they realize that this isn't the case.

You should throw yourself totally into your business, putting in long hours of hard work. This may be difficult at first, but the rewards for this hard work will make it all seem worthwhile. You should be entering into this new venture with enthusiasm, energy, excitement, and the will to give it your best shot.

Remember, selling is a complicated business, involving many skills that you must acquire if you are to succeed. It is only when you take it seriously, that you begin on the road to success.

Constantly evaluate your work. Stand back and look at what you're doing, see if you can find any room for improvement; then you will be moving towards becoming the completely finished article.

You should be positive and enthusiastic about your product or service, and eager to demonstrate to the customer how it will help him. You must also have complete knowledge about your product, because without it you will lack confidence in yourself. If you are unable to answer customer queries about what you're offering, he will lose confidence and trust in you, and that is the road to failure.

Always be looking for new customers. If you are unable to find new prospects to hopefully turn into customers, your business will cease to grow.

Your ability to manage your time effectively is of vital importance. You should plan and organize yourself so as to ensure that your days are spent carrying out the crucial tasks that drive your business forward, and not on trivial pursuits. If you continue to manage your time ineffectively, your sales will fall below what is required to keep your business afloat.

To ensure that your company grows, you must continue to improve your performance in each important area. Therefore you should constantly monitor your performance in every part of the sale; from the prospecting, right through to the close. It is attention to these details that will determine whether or not you succeed. If you carry out all these tasks well, you will definitely succeed. If you do them not so well, you will struggle to succeed. Even if you only do some well, this still isn't really good enough. You must aspire to achieve excellence, and do your utmost to achieve this. If you succeed, you will become a top salesperson.

Top salespeople are seen by their customers as friends. The customer values their advice when making buying decisions. He has total faith in the fact that whatever they suggest will be his best interests, and not just for the sake of a quick sale.

Being able to stand back and honestly analyze your ability in all the key areas of selling takes a lot of courage; but if you have the drive in you to do this, and are determined to improve in your lacking areas, you will dramatically improve your sales.

You must be willing to do whatever it takes to achieve your

full potential in selling, and put in as much time, effort and money as is necessary. You should be prepared to put into this venture whatever it takes to succeed.

Your desire for excellence must be so strong that it will spur you on, through both the good times and the bad, the fears and the doubts, and the problems and the set-backs. Be absolutely clear about what you want to achieve; this is essential if you want to succeed. You should also be clear about what you are selling, and who you are selling it to. Know who your competition is, and what they offer their customers; and then try to better what they offer.

Work on building-up your confidence, this will help you to conquer the doubts and uncertainties that all salespeople encounter from time to time. Confidence comes from knowing every detail about what you are selling, and knowing that it is exactly what the customer needs. If you are comfortable with every aspect of your selling, this signal is picked-up by the customer, and he will feel much more positive about doing business with you. Above all, confidence comes from your total belief that you are giving the customer something that is best suited to his specific needs.

Always set yourself the highest standards in every aspect of your work, and then be tenacious in your effort to achieve these standards. Remember, you will never get any more out of your business than you put into it. But what you do put in, you will definitely get back, and more besides.

Chapter 23

WHAT MOTIVATES A CUSTOMER TO BUY?

The way to motivate a customer to buy is to convince him how much better off he will be if he purchases your product or service. The perceived wisdom is that customers don't buy products or services; instead they buy solutions to problems, or something to help them achieve their aims or improve their lives. In short, if the customer thinks his future will be more desirable by purchasing your product, this will motivate him to do so.

The desire to obtain and the fear of losing out are the main drives behind most buying decisions. You should structure your advertising so as to always include both these motivators.

To establish high levels of goodwill, you must do things that are more than what the customer expects. This can lead to referrals, resales and testimonials; all of which are essential for your success in sales.

Doing more than what the customer expects, and going out of your way to be more accommodating are excellent ways of building long-term customer relationships. This extra effort will both amaze and please your customer, and leave him wanting to do more business with you.

Your product or service must be the most appropriate, and

suit the customers needs; as well as being the solution to his problems. The quality of your product must be of a high enough standard to enable it to meet the customer's needs. It is not the high quality of your product or service that motivates customers to buy, but rather, whether or not it is the very best solution to his problems.

Customers nowadays require and expect the very best quality at the most attractive price. If the customer thinks that your not providing good value, you will lose his business, and he will look elsewhere for someone who can.

You must show how your customer's circumstances will improve after ordering your product or service; and how they will miss-out on all the benefits it has to offer if they do not buy it. You must also explain how the benefits of your product or service far exceed those of your competitors, and how he will actually save money in the long-term by ordering it.

From the customer's point of view, the major factor that concerns him is the usefulness of your product or service. Will it do what he wants it to do? You will rarely find that price is the reason why customers buy. They assume that the price of your product or service will be fair and honest. They simply expect to be charged a reasonable price. You can never entice someone to buy something that he does not want or need by simply cutting the price. Price reductions rarely motivate people to buy. Customers buy because you have demonstrated the advantages of your product sufficiently; and shown that it meets their specific needs. Your job is to satisfy the customer that your product or service will fulfil his needs in a much better way than anything that your competitors are offering.

A prospective customer wants a knowledgeable and well-informed salesperson to assist him in making a good buying decision. He simply wants to know the truth about a product or service; how it will improve his present situation and also benefit him in the future. He wants you to assist him in making the right decision; but without putting him under any pressure. In the end, he likes to make his own mind up.

Customers will buy from someone with whom they feel comfortable, rather than someone who made them feel apprehensive or pressurized. Your skill in creating a positive impression on your customer; coupled with the feeling that he can have complete trust in the reliability of both you and your product is crucial to your business success.

Do That Little Bit More
Always look for ways in which you can improve what you're doing. Never see yourself as a person who is so proficient at what you do that you can rest on your laurels. You should be asking yourself if your customers are completely satisfied with the product or service you provide. What could you do to attract more customers to your website? What little extras could you provide to give you the edge over your competitors? Compare yourself to the most successful salespeople, and ask yourself what they are doing that is different from you; and when you find out what it is, make a conscious effort to do the same, or even more. This is the way to become successful.

Create A Good Impression
It is important that you build and maintain the trust of your customers. They must believe in both you and your product or service. The smallest detail can sometimes start to sow the seeds of doubt in a customer's mind. Even down to something as simple and trivial as the quality of your business cards. So, don't make the mistake of printing your business cards on thin paper. If your business card is substandard, the customer will assume that your business and your product is too. On the other hand, a crisp, hard,

substantial business card will give the impression that you and your product are substantial also.

Customers are quick to form opinions about salespeople; and once they have formed their opinion, they tend to stick to it. So, bearing this in mind, it cannot be stressed strongly enough how important it is for you to create a good impression at the very beginning.

You must see your most important job as a salesman as being to build and maintain a strong relationship with your customers. You must ensure that everything you do causes him to feel at ease and confident in dealing with you. He must also feel totally positive about buying your product or service. This is achieved by showing him how your product will allow him to get what he really wants and needs in order to improve his life or work.

The best type of prospect is someone who has an urgent need for the type of product or service you are selling. Or someone who has a problem that your product would readily solve. The more prospects you can obtain that have an urgent need for your product or service, the more successful you will be.

You should take every opportunity to demonstrate to the prospect that buying your product or service will benefit him to such an extent that it would be extremely unwise not to proceed.

A customer that you have already sold to in the past is a good potential prospect. He will already have had a good experience with you and your products, and will be positive and receptive to what you are currently offering. You will find it very easy to persuade him about the benefits and advantages of your present product because he has done business with you in the past; and these past experiences have given him a huge amount of trust in you.

Make good use of your time. You will only be successful in sales by dealing with prospects that can be persuaded into purchasing your products or services. And, then hopefully turning these prospects into regular customers. The quality of your prospects will have an impact on your sales targets.

Customers have reasons for both buying and not buying. It's vital that you arrange, in order of priority, the reasons why a customer should purchase your product or service; and incorporate these reasons into your sales literature and on your website.

Highlight the areas in which your product or service is superior to that of your competitors. From the customer's point of view, this is one of the most important things to bear in mind when deciding which company they should do business with.

Use Your Time Wisely
Bear in mind, your time is precious. Dealing with awkward customers isn't the best use of your time. They are usually very hard work for very scant reward. It's probably best to just avoid them, if possible.

You should organize your time so you spend more time with good prospects. This is an excellent way to increase your sales; and not only that, you will also find it far more rewarding. It will make you feel much more positive about yourself and your product or service.

Referrals from satisfied customers is an excellent source for obtaining new business. They are quite literally worth their weight in gold. When you are recommended to a customer by someone he knows, it saves you both the time and effort of having to build the trust and credibility that you would have to do if you were starting from scratch.

Coping With Rejection

Do not be disheartened by a negative response from prospects. You are bound to experience these over the course of your career in selling. The important thing to remember is that rejection is not a personal attack on you, nor a reflection on your product or service. It's probably just that the customer has no need for what you're offering him at that moment in time. No matter how good your product or service is, you can never avoid being rejected at some point. But you must do your utmost to reduce the number of rejections you receive. Try to learn something from your rejections, so that you will be better equipped to handle this type of situation the next time it occurs.

In order to make a prospect more receptive to buying your product or service, you must reveal a need or problem that he has. Once you have done this, you then show him how your product will be the solution to his need or problem. You must convince him that buying your product or service will be the wisest choice to make, both in terms of saving him money and solving his problems. Lastly, you must obtain a commitment from him to buy.

Don't assume that just because you have proven that the prospect will be better off with your product or service, he will necessarily buy it. He may need what you're selling, but he may think that his need is not sufficient enough to warrant buying. You must convince him that buying your product or service is the best possible choice he could make, and that his situation will improve dramatically as a result of purchasing it.

You must show him how much his present situation will improve by using your product or service. He must be made to recognize that he has a need which is unfulfilled, or a problem that is unresolved at the present time; but that by owning and using what you are offering, he could be much better off.

Some customers may treat you with suspicion and scepticism. This is probably due to the fact that they have been sold faulty or shoddy goods in the past; and are therefore extremely cautious in case the same thing happens again. They will be suspicious about how much of what you say about your product or service is actually true. They will be cautious in case you are making exaggerated claims about your product in order to get them to buy. In cases like this, where the prospect is suspicious and wary of you, the best way to allay his fears and suspicions is to show him that other people have used your product or service, and have been happy with the results. This is the time when testimonials from previous customers are vital to your success.

Trustworthiness
Remember, you need to be extremely plausible and trustworthy before a customer will even consider buying from you. But they may be persuaded by knowing that other people in similar situations to theirs have purchased your product and have had no regrets in doing so. This is why testimonials are so crucial to sales success. Without them you can lose out on a large amount of business. In many cases, an excellent testimonial is all it takes to make the sale. The best type of testimonials are those from people in a similar situation to your prospect.

Once you have acquired the necessary skills to convince the customer that your product or service can solve his problems cost effectively, you are on your way to success in sales.

It's possible that your prospect may decide to shop around before he decides whether or not your product or service is indeed the best solution to his problem. This is when you should introduce your trump card, your most formidable weapon, the area where you have the advantage over your competitors. This is commonly knows as the U.S.P. (Unique Selling Proposition). Let your prospect know exactly what your particular product does that gives it the advantage over what your competitors are offering.

Sometimes it can be difficult to distinguish between what a customer wants and what he needs. Just because the customer wants your product or service; it doesn't automatically follow that he needs it. In instances like this, you must do your utmost to convince the customer that the reason why he wants your product or service is actually due to the fact that he realises deep down inside that he needs it too.

Persuasion

Customers buy products or services either to acquire something desirable, or because they fear that they might lose out on something if they don't. A good technique you can employ in your advertising and on your website is to use certain phrases which motivate the customer into making a buying decision. These can be phrases such as: "When you own this product you will see the benefits straight away." This type of advertising is extremely effective.

Another phrase you can use is: "If you purchase this today, we will despatch it immediately, so that you can start enjoying the benefits within a few short days." Once a person has decided to order something, speed of delivery becomes a matter of great urgency to them. Customers want things immediately; they don't like the thought of having to wait an unnecessarily long time to receive their goods. The speed with which you can deliver your goods is a crucial driving force for him to commit to buying.

Another motivational phrase you can use is: "As soon as you start using it, you will notice the difference straight away." Your purpose here is get your customer to visualise himself enjoying the benefits of using your product. This will make him far more susceptible to buying what you offer.

Product Knowledge

Your measure of success will depend upon your product knowledge. You must know every detail about the product or service you offer; what exactly does it do? how exactly does it work, and what are the various tasks it can perform?

It's always advantageous if you familiarize yourself with your competitor's products also, so you know precisely what you're up against. Make it your number one priority to become totally proficient in the field of the product or service that you sell. You must be determined never to find yourself in the situation where you are unable to answer a question about your product or service. If this happens you will quickly lose the confidence of the customer, and almost certainly lose the sale as well.

When describing the features that your product or service offers, you should also let the customer know how he benefits from them, and how much better off he will be by using your product. You must always connect together the features of your product or service with the benefits that the customer will gain by using it.

You will more than likely lose the sale if you demonstrate to the customer the benefits of your product or service, but neglect to inform him of the benefits that he will enjoy from using it. You must be extremely thorough, and leave nothing to chance. Sometimes it can be the inclusion of one small detail that makes the sale. But, on the other hand, it can be the omission of one minor detail that can lose it.

Chapter 24

HONESTY

Your job is to turn a suspicious prospect into a trusting customer. Try your utmost to convert them into a high-quality customer, with whom you can have a long-standing relationship.

Selling isn't easy. Once you accept the fact that selling is a difficult profession, it will become less stressful. Take some comfort from the fact that even for the most experienced salespeople, it can be hard. But, on the other hand, the rewards can be great. Your earning potential from this profession can be astronomical. This is why you should persist. Remember, if selling was easy, everyone would be doing it; and your potential earnings would be significantly reduced. So, maybe you should be thankful that selling is difficult. Also, bear in mind that, in this profession you could eventually become financially independent.

Your main aim, throughout all your dealings with the customer, is to help him solve his problems, or accomplish his aims. Convince him that your product or service will do both these things. If you succeed in doing this, and your customer is happy with his purchase, this should leave him wanting to do further business with you; and you can build and maintain a good relationship together.

Never try to influence the customer to do something that is not in his best interests. If you want to build and maintain the trust of your customer, you must only steer him into making the buying decision that is best for him.

Customers can sometimes be suspicious and sceptical of salespeople. This may be because they have had bad experiences in the past. They may have been sold shoddy goods, and are afraid of making the same mistake again. They have built up a mistrust of salespeople to the point where they will disbelieve and treat with caution any claims you make about your product or service. This fear of making the mistake of buying sub-standard goods again is the main reason for their reluctance to commit to making a buying decision.

Other customers have become comfortable with their present situation, and are therefore reluctant to make any changes; even if it is to their advantage. They probably realize that they would be better off with your product or service; but they really don't want to go through all the trouble and upheaval of switching over to someone new. They just can't be bothered to make the effort.

Chapter 25

PRICE

Your major priority throughout the course of the sales process is to convince the customer that, in terms of the value to them of what you're offering; the price you're charging is negligible.

Always be enthusiastic about what you are selling. You must have total belief that what you are selling is a good, high quality product. If you don't believe in what you sell, your disbelief may be picked-up by the customer. It is only when the customer is as enthusiastic about your product or service as you are, that the sale can proceed.

You should always put the interests of the customer before your own personal interest of making the sale. Customers can detect when someone is being insincere and only thinking about what's in it for himself. The customer will become defensive when he suspects this, and immediately lose interest; and you will lose the sale.

Be professional at all times. Never put the customer under any pressure; or do anything that can be interpreted as being manipulative. This will only serve to damage the already fragile relationship you are trying to develop. All dealings with your customer must be honest, sincere, and above all else, always in his best interests. Never attempt to control or influence his choice in a way that could be construed as manipulation. Let him make up his own mind.

The customer should be made aware that goods of higher quality are bound to cost a bit more; but that superior quality goods often end up saving people money in the long term. Customers are unlikely to pay more for your product or service if your competitors are offering what appears to be a similar product, but at a lower price. In these instances you should show the customer how your product is superior to that of your competitors. This should be enough to persuade him that the extra benefits he will enjoy from owning your product more than compensates for the price. Prolonged reluctance to buy, due to concerns over the price are a clear indication that you haven't convinced the customer about the benefits of owning your product or service.

Some customers simply need to learn a few home truths, such as:

> You only get what pay for in life.
> You don't get something for nothing.
> You don't get something good for a cheap price.

The majority of people know from past experiences that, whenever they try to save money by buying cheaper goods; they invariably end up regretting it.

You must be completely committed to gaining the trust of your customer, to the point where he has no doubt that you are acting in his best interests. You must also build his confidence in you by proving yourself to be informed, capable, friendly and helpful. All this has to happen before he will be willing to proceed.

When the customer does agree to buy, he is entirely dependent on you to fulfil your promises. And, if you want to develop a friendly relationship in which the customer likes you and knows he can completely rely on you; you must ensure that you do fulfil the commitments you have made, or even exceed them.

Most refusals to buy are due to the fact that the customer doesn't have complete trust in you. To overcome this, you must do everything in your power to prove to him that you are completely competent and reliable. Leave him feeling sufficiently confident in your trustworthiness and integrity. It is extremely important that you do this, as more sales are lost due to customer's lack of trust than for almost any other reason. This isn't surprising when you look at things from the customer's point of view. You're asking him for a substantial amount of money, so it isn't surprising if he feels some concern or anxiety. When you think about it, it's only natural if he doubts whether he's making the right decision; or if he'll regret it eventually, wouldn't you?

Let the customer feel as though he is making up his own mind. By all means guide him by giving him good advice in order to help him make the right decision. But he should be left in no doubt that he has made the best possible choice by deciding to buy your product.

Chapter 26

CUSTOMER REQUIREMENTS

In order to bring the sales process to a satisfactory conclusion, you must satisfy the customer on the following points:

<u>Does The Customer Want What You're Selling?</u>

The customer must be convinced beyond any doubt that he does require what you are offering.

<u>Does The Customer Trust You?</u>

The customer must have confidence in you, and believe that you are capable of satisfying all his requirements. He should be convinced that you are totally reliable and trustworthy.

<u>Does The Customer Need The Product Or Service You're Selling?</u>

The customer should be left in no doubt that your product or service will assist him in solving his problems and achieving his goals cost effectively. But, and this cannot be stressed strongly enough, you too must believe that buying your product is in the customer's best interests.

Does The Customer Know Exactly What He's Buying?

It must be made crystal clear to the customer exactly what he will receive when he purchases your product or service. It is your responsibility to ensure that the customer completely understands what he has bought and how it will work.

Don't make false claims about your product or service. Since trust and confidence are essential ingredients to a successful sale, you would be foolish to do anything that might jeopardize something so precious. When you say that your product or service can do something that you clearly know it cannot, it is almost tantamount to misrepresentation. Remember, honesty is always the best policy.

You are more likely to get repeat business and referrals if you are seen as a reliable and trustworthy salesperson than if you are viewed upon as someone who has a tendency to exaggerate or make false claims about your products.

Remember to ask for the order after you have demonstrated all the features and benefits of your product or service. If you don't, you are giving the customer time to change his mind; or maybe forget why he was so enthusiastic to purchase it in the first place.

Chapter 27

TAKE IT SERIOUSLY

If you follow the steps outlined in this book there is no reason why you shouldn't succeed in becoming a professional salesperson. But you do have to take it seriously because you are dealing with products and services that may be vital to other people's lives or businesses. You must continue to acquire more skills and gain more product knowledge on a daily basis. You must develop the attitude that you are going to succeed, and that there can be no thought of failure; you are going to persist and you are going to succeed.

There are bound to be some setbacks in the early stages, but you must keep on going. Believe in yourself and in your ability to deal with every problem. Bear in mind that each failure will bring you a little bit closer to success.

Keep on going! Remember you haven't failed until you say to yourself "I give up!" Failures count for absolutely nothing if you succeed in the end.

Prioritise Your Tasks
If, like the majority of people nowadays, you are inundated by work and tasks that continue to mount-up, you will constantly find yourself with a backlog of work. You will probably never have enough time to catch-up on all the tasks.

If this is the case, it is important that you begin prioritising your tasks by selecting the most important ones, and starting on them first; ensuring that you complete them satisfactorily before you begin any others. If you do this, you will be amazed at the results you can achieve. But you must do this continuously if you want to get to the top. The secret to achieving high levels of performance and output is for you to complete your major tasks fully and professionally before even contemplating doing anything else. You must get into the habit of doing this every day so that it becomes an automatic routine.

One of the best ways of building a successful career is by developing the habit of finishing important tasks. But they must be the most important jobs. You will only be wasting your time if you do the jobs that need not be done at all.

Constantly set yourself targets and deadlines. This will give you a greater sense of urgency; because without a specific deadline, there will be a lack of motivation and clarity, and you will achieve very little.

Think seriously about what you are going to have to do to achieve success. Take time out to sit down and plan what you need to do first, and what can be put off till later. Make a list of what you need to do in order to obtain the best results. Form a list of individual tasks you will need to do to accomplish this. You will find that a written list of what needs to be done, and in what order will help you become far more productive. Clearly written goals are a great motivational force.

Always plan your day in advance. You'll be surprised at how much time this can actually save you. Make a list the night before of the important tasks that need to be completed the next day. People find that they achieve far more when they are working from a well prepared list.

As you go through the day completing your tasks, cross them

off your list. This will give you a great feeling of achievement. Set out your list in order of priority. You will often find that one item on your list can be far more beneficial to you and your business than all the other ones combined. This is the task that must be tackled first.

Do The Important Jobs First
The most crucial tasks are often the most difficult and intricate ones.

But the benefits you will gain from completing these can be enormous. Sometimes it can be very difficult to motivate yourself to begin a vital task; but once you actually start on it, you invariably find yourself committed to seeing it through to the end. Your ability to determine what tasks are more important than others will be a major factor in determining whether or not you succeed.

Remember, something important will have more of an impact on your business than something unimportant. So always ensure that you not only do the most important jobs first; but that you always do them to the very best of your ability.

Your ability to set out tasks according to their priority, and tirelessly see them through to completion is a proven way to ensure your success. When you acquire this invaluable skill, there are virtually no limits to what you can achieve.

When you have definite goals, you know exactly what you want to achieve. Your skill at determining what you want to accomplish in every area of your business is vital to your success.

One of the most common reasons why people fail in business is because they waste too much of their time doing tasks that are of little, or no value whatsoever. In the majority of cases, the reason why they waste so much valuable time is because they just have no idea what they really want. When you have specific goals, your proficiency in managing your time effectively improves considerably.

Once you get into the habit of doing those tasks that propel you towards your goal, your business will soar. You will see a marked improvement in your results; to the extent that you will probably no longer have the time to spend on tasks that aren't important. Before you begin any task, you should always bear in mind what the consequences of doing, or not doing it are. The things that matter most must never be neglected or replaced by the things of little or no importance.

Always take the long-term view of your business, rather than giving little, or no thought to the future. People who have a clear vision of where they want their business to go are able to make much better judgements regarding use of their time; and are more effective than people who only think in the short-term. Having a clear vision of what you want to achieve in the long-term enables you to make better short-term decisions. Successful people tend to be those who make sacrifices in the short term so they can reap the rewards in the long-term. Whereas unsuccessful people tend to give little, or no thought to the future.

Be single-minded in your endeavours to continually complete the vital tasks that will benefit both you and your company first. This way you will be constantly moving towards your goals. The more time you spend on planning and setting priorities, the more vital tasks you will complete; and in a much faster time.

One major cause of procrastination is due to the fact that many people tend to put off the jobs that they don't feel very confident doing. If there are areas where you have performed not so well in the past, instead of avoiding these, you should make the effort to improve in that particular area. If you don't, the situation will only get worse. Set yourself a goal to improve in these areas. You never know, the difference between whether or not you succeed in business may be down to your proficiency in one of these vital skills. Just remember, if you apply yourself in the correct way, you can acquire any business skill. People aren't born with business skills, they acquire them, often through hard work.

You will get far more work done, and in a faster time if you become proficient in your vital task areas. This is a very important point to bear in mind; as it could have a major impact on the future of your business.

You'll find that there is never enough time to get everything done, but there is always sufficient time during the day to get the vital tasks completed. This means that you will never be on top of all the tasks that need doing, so don't even bother trying to complete them all. The best you can hope for is to be able to start and finish the most important jobs. Always ensure that you use your time wisely; if you do you will become a highly productive person. The key to your success in business is your ability to determine which tasks should be given the highest priority; and then to start on these activities immediately.

Know Your Product
Product knowledge is vitally important to success in business. You should be continually improving your knowledge about your product, and also your competitors products. This will improve your confidence and help you excel in what you do. Otherwise you will feed inadequate, lack confidence, and have little or no faith in your ability to do your job.

Self improvement is one of the best ways to save time. The more proficient and confident you are in your work, the more you relish the job in hand. You will become enthusiastic about your work, and because of this you will get a lot more done in a shorter period of time. This is true, when you know that you can do your job well, you naturally tend to get the job done better and faster.

Never allow a perceived inability in some area of your work discourage you or hold you back. All business skills are attainable. If others have managed to learn them, then you can too. Set about learning whatever skills are necessary for you to become more productive and effective.

One additional skill that you learn can make a huge difference to how you do your job. So, you should continually learn new skills that will give you the edge over your competitors.

Continually gaining product knowledge will help you feel strong, confident and enthusiastic about what you do; and customers will pick-up on those feelings. Enthusiasm is contagious. If you are passionate about what you sell, your customers will be carried along by the strength of your conviction.

One Step At A Time

What unique talents do you have that you can use to your advantage? What are you especially good at? Take some time to think about what specialized skills you have that you can utilise in your work. These will invariably be the tasks in which you excel, and that give you the most satisfaction.

Remember, your main aim in business is to acquire customers. Once you obtain these customers, you must do everything in your power to keep them. If you do this effectively, you will increase your profit and your company will grow.

Determine exactly what the most crucial part of your business is. Which tasks, if completed effectively, would have the most positive impact on your business. Once you know the answer to this question, you should immediately take action and ensure that these tasks are dealt with.

Never allow yourself to be daunted by the size of the task that lies ahead of you. The most effective way to avoid becoming overwhelmed is to do one task at a time. No matter how big the list of tasks in front of you may seem to be, just concentrate on doing one vital task, and see it through to completion. Just by developing the habit of starting and completing one task, and then moving on the next and so on, you will soon realize that you can accomplish more than you thought was possible.

To be successful you must continually push yourself to perform at the highest level. You should always aim to perform at the highest standards and try to go that little bit further, or do more than is necessary or expected. Set deadlines for yourself and make sure you always meet them. By exerting this sort of pressure on yourself, you achieve more and you complete your tasks quicker than you were previously able to. This in turn builds-up your confidence, and you feel more motivated and enthused about tackling your workload. You quickly develop the habit of completing all your vital tasks, which makes you a far more efficient performer.

When you suffer the inevitable setbacks and difficulties that occur when you run a business, never let them dishearten you; always try your best to remain optimistic. Try to find something good or advantageous to salvage from a difficult situation. If you look hard enough, you can usually find something useful to learn from most bad experiences.

Always look at ways in which you can solve your problems. Instead of moaning and whining when things go wrong, devote your time and energy into the valuable task of solving the problem. You won't achieve anything by wasting time complaining about it.

Constantly think about how you're going to achieve your goals, and what you hope to accomplish in the future. Always look at the road ahead, and not in the rear view mirror. Keep yourself focused on moving forward towards a better future; and on what you must do to improve your life and your business. This will have the effect of making you feel much more positive and give you the incentive you need to get started on your vital tasks. It will also make you more determined keep on going, through the good times, and the bad.

Continually go over your duties in order to determine which time-consuming tasks you can safely avoid. These will invariably be the activities that are of little, or no benefit to you or your company. This will have the advantage of giving you more time to devote to the really important tasks that will move your business forward.

Don't be overwhelmed by the size of the job ahead. A good method to employ when you are faced with large jobs that fill you with dread due to their size, is to do them one small section at a time. You do this by looking over the whole task in detail, and then separating it into smaller parts. Once you have done this, you then set about completing these smaller sections one at a time. You will find it noticeably easier to complete a small section of a large job; rather than trying to do the whole thing in one go. This is far more productive than you would imagine, before you know it, the task will be completed.

Time Management
Another method you can employ to deal with huge tasks is to spend a specific amount of time each day on them. This can be as small a time period as you feel comfortable with, maybe as little as a few minutes. You decide how much time you spend on this task; and when you feel as though you've had enough, you simply stop and do something else.

Both these techniques are very easy to employ. You'll find them very useful, especially when you're faced with a task that you previously would have considered to be overwhelming.

Continually look for ways in which you can save yourself time. Plan your day ahead by choosing each vital task that needs to be done, and the amount of time you wish to spend on each of these tasks. Be sure to devote your time only on important tasks; the ones that will have the most substantive long-term effects.

Spend your time wisely. Plan and prepare all your tasks in advance, and then launch yourself quickly into them. You should have a clear objective of what your goals and objectives are for each day; and you must work tirelessly to complete them. If you work steadily and continuously in this manner, you'll be amazed at the amount of work you get through.

Your skill in determining your vital tasks and then completing them tenaciously and accurately, is the crucial ingredient needed to ensure your success. The key to high productivity lies in your ability to choose a vital task that needs to be undertaken first; and your dogged determination that you will not stop until this task is completed. Once you've mastered this simple technique, you'll be amazed at the effect it will have on your business, but more especially the effect it has on you. It increases your enthusiasm and motivation. You feel more energetic, and you gain a great deal of satisfaction in seeing your workload gradually decreasing while your business moves forward. Working non-stop on one task at a time means you get more work done in less time. You become more resolute in your self-belief; and you feel more confident and happy as you see yourself develop into someone who is far more competent and productive. Once you acquire the habit of starting on your most important task prior to all the others, there is no reason why you shouldn't succeed. But, you will only succeed if you adhere to these principles regularly and steadfastly.

Just to clarify, your most important tasks and priorities are the ones that, if not completed quickly and satisfactorily can, and often do have the gravest consequences on your business.

What separates a truly professional person from an average one is the time that he takes to prepare. The person who isn't entirely serious often attempts to struggle through with a minimum amount of preparation.

The more eager to succeed you become, the more likely it is that you will be compelled to work to the maximum of your ability on the tasks that are most crucial to your business. This will inevitably guarantee that you do become successful. And the more successful you become, the busier you will become; and you'll discover that there is never enough time to complete all your tasks. When faced with this situation, you must always remember that there is never enough time to get everything done, but there is always time to get the important things done. You usually find out the hard way how much you can do; and you determine this by trying to do too much. Only by stretching yourself to your absolute limits can you discover what you are capable of achieving.

For you to be totally successful, you must work to the very limits of your ability. But, if you truly love what you're doing, this will be less of a challenge.

Persistence is an absolute necessity if you are to succeed in business; it is an invaluable asset to have. If you are able to keep on going, even when faced with the inevitable temporary setbacks you are bound to experience from time to time; this will prove that you have the right temperament to succeed. Your success will be guaranteed if you unrelentingly pursue your goals with dogged determination and an unshakable resolve never to give up.

KEEP REMINDING YOURSELF THAT FAILURE ISN'T IN YOUR VOCABULARY!

Chapter 28

CUSTOMER SATISFACTION

Your main function in business is to create customers. Once you have achieved this, your next function should be to make sure that you hang onto them. Your level of sales will be directly attributable to how successful you are at doing this.

Always be on the lookout for ways to make your company more successful. Ask yourself the following:

> Who and where are my best customers?
>
> What can I do that's different from my competitors?
>
> What is my unique selling proposition?
>
> Who are my most profitable customers?
>
> What can I do to attract more customers like these?
>
> How can I identify the areas where I can create and keep new customers?
>
> Are there any opportunities for me to publicize new products or services?
>
> Can I build upon the loyalty of my customers?

The most successful companies continually look for ways to satisfy their customers. Even when they succeed in this, they still look for ways to improve upon the service they provide. This is how you stay ahead of the competition. Always give your customers the very best service that you are capable of. Continually aim to exceed your customer's expectations. Constantly ask yourself what you could offer your customers that goes beyond what your competitors offer. The effect this will have on your business will be amazing. Not only will customers keep on buying from you; but they will advise others to buy from you also.

The customer will always endeavour to get what they want as easily and quickly as possible, and for the lowest possible price. If you cannot offer them all of this, they will simply go to someone who can.

In order to keep hold of your customers you should constantly be looking at ways to increase the amount of effort you put into satisfying his desires and needs. Always leave the customer feeling happy and relieved that he chose your company.

Customers will inevitably seek to fulfil their greatest number of desires or needs when they contemplate buying from you. It's the companies that provide the highest quality products at the lowest possible prices that survive in today's climate.

For customers to perceive your company as high in quality, you must be able to offer them the assurance that you can cater for their overriding need for safety and peace of mind. They need to be sure of this before they make a purchasing decision.

When having to make a choice between products or services of a higher or lower price, depending upon their financial situation, customers will usually choose the higher priced product because they believe that the higher the price, the better the quality. If the customer believes that he is purchasing high quality goods, he assumes that they will be of a superior standard, and therefore more reliable. He feels he is taking less or a risk, and this makes his decision to buy much easier.

Try To Do More
To be successful you should continually be introducing new products and services. Always be thinking along the lines of improving your business; and when you have thought of these new ideas and innovations, choose the ones that have the greatest earning potential.

Examine in detail the direction in which your business is heading.

    Are sales increasing or declining?

    What do customers require more or less of?

    What lines should you keep; and which should you drop?

Keep a close eye on what your main competitors are doing.

    In what areas are they surpassing you?

    What are they doing that you could also do?

To excel in business, you must perform to a very high standard in the following areas: product quality, service, distribution and marketing. If you perform badly in any of these key areas, your business could, and most probably would struggle to survive. A weakness in any of your key areas could seriously hamper your chances of reaching the standard required for long term success.

To achieve the highest standards, you must analyze your critical tasks, and how well you perform at them. If you feel that there is room for improvement, you should develop a strategy to become better and more proficient in that area.

Your knowledge and skills are a determining factor to your success. But, on the other hand, your deficiencies in certain critical areas can limit what you are capable of achieving. You must discover your areas of deficiency, and what skills you need to improve upon to ensure your success. Exactly what skills, if you improved significantly would have the best possible impact on your business? When you find the answer to this question, you should immediately set about developing these skills. This is what successful people do; and this is why they are so successful.

Don't be deterred by the thought of failure. Remember, all great successes were preceded by failures; sometimes a great many failures. But every failure contains an invaluable lesson that you can learn from. Your task is to determine what these lessons are.

You should be continually striving to better yourself, because there will always be room for improvement. Remember, if you stand still too long your competitors will catch up on you, and eventually overtake you. You should determine what your strengths are, and crucially, what your weaknesses are. When your identify your weaknesses, you usually find the cause of most of your problems.

Draw-up a strategy to become completely competent in at least one vital area that will help both you and your business; and don't be satisfied until you have completely mastered this crucial skill.

Success in business is dependent upon your ability to compete against your rivals in today's world. With this in mind, you should always keep a lookout for new and innovative products and services; or for ways you can improve upon what you already offer.

There must be no doubt in the customer's mind about what your product is capable of doing, or who it is designed for. If he isn't sure about what your product does, or what benefit it will be to him, he will simply disregard it completely.

Find Your Niche Market

What is your niche market?

What exactly are you offering?

Who is your customer?

What does your customer consider to be good value?

What explicit needs or desires does your customer have; and will your product or service satisfy them?

These are vitally important questions that you should constantly be asking yourself. You also need to know:

How can your product or service be improved upon in order to fulfil the desires and needs of a greater amount of customers?

How can you make your product or service more attractive to a wider market without losing any of your regular customers, or jeopardizing your unique niche market?

The customer needs to know what it is that makes your product unique or different from what your competitors are offering. It needs to have special attributes that single it out from similar products on the market.

For you to succeed in business, your product or service must be distinctive and have qualities that make it superior to what your competitors are offering. If your product or service has unique features, this will give you a distinct advantage over the other companies that are competing for your share of the marketplace.

So, in order to give yourself a competitive advantage you must ensure that your product or service is superior to that of your competitors.

You should also determine why your customers buy from you, rather than from somebody else. Try to get some feedback from them about what it is they like best about the service you provide. This perceived difference between you and your competitors is what will give you the competitive advantage over them. If you don't currently have a definable competitive advantage of any sort, you should immediately set about developing one.

You must aim your product or service at particular customer groups, or one specific area of the market. This defined area will contain those customers who will benefit the most from what you have to offer.

Once you have established exactly who your customers are, you should determine precisely how to sell your product or service to them; because your success depends upon your ability to sell to this niche market you have located.

Chapter 29

STANDARDS OF EXCELLENCE

Customers want the very best products for the lowest price. They also want high quality products or services because these are usually more reliable and tend to satisfy more explicit needs. Once you have established a reputation for supplying products or services of high quality at a reasonable price, your success in business is guaranteed.

Speed of service is also a major factor in the customer's perception. So, it would also be advantageous if you could build a reputation as being someone who is constantly trying to do things better and faster.

Remember, your must have a product or service that people want, need and are favourably disposed towards paying for. If what you are selling is not ideally suited to the specific needs of your niche market, you must quickly adapt to meet these needs; otherwise customers will abandon you and look for someone who's products better suits their requirements.

You should never stop learning and looking for ways to improve both yourself and your business. Continually moving forward and focusing on elevating yourself towards achieving bigger and better things will be a major factor in your quest to gain the competitive advantage which is essential for long-term business success.

Customers will be more favourably disposed towards you and your product if they see you as someone who is completely reliable. They must have every confidence in the fact that you will do exactly what you have promised. They must trust you implicitly and know that you will always keep to your word. If you live your life adhering to high moral principles, you will feel much better about yourself. This rule not only applies to your business: but your personal life also.

Be Optimistic

One of the most potent qualities for success in business is optimism. Optimistic people believe they can achieve great things and are continually striving to do just that. They look for the positive in every situation; and when something does go wrong, they find some good to take from that problem or setback and look upon it as a learning and growing experience. If any problem crops up, far from fearing or avoiding it, they see it as an enticing challenge and resolve to tackle it. They have no concerns about taking risks, which is why they are invariably so successful. They don't fear failure because, as they see it, failures are inevitable stepping stones on the road to success. If you can view each setback as a learning experience that will eventually lead you to certain success, you will become a far more effective businessman and achieve all of your goals.

How you respond to the inevitable problems that will arise will be a true test of your resilience. Business life, just like life in general is a constant succession of problems and troublesome situations. When these occur, you should stay calm, take stock of the situation and immediately begin a plan of action to remedy the situation. If you're able to stay focused, you will usually find the best course of action to take.

Always bear in mind that there can be no success without the inevitable and unavoidable failure. Whether or not you're capable of dealing with these problems will be a crucial factor in determining how far you progress in business.

Choose The Right Product

You must believe in what you are selling. If you don't have faith in your product or service, you will find it very difficult, if not almost impossible to persuade the customer that it is right for him. Many salespeople have found that by switching to another product or service that they truly believe in, they have gone from strength to strength.

So, be certain that your product is right for the customer and also right for you. The product must suit the customer, he must need it, want it, and benefit from using it. If all these criteria are met, a successful sale can take place.

Remember, when your customer is considering purchasing your product or service, he is looking for something that will solve his problems or make his life easier. You must be able to ascertain if your product can do both these things effectively.

Ask yourself the following questions about your product or service:-

> Will it fulfil the needs and desires of your customer?
>
> Will it improve his life?
>
> Will he benefit from using it?

Your job is to unearth needs and problems that the customer already has; not invent false needs just to sell your product or service. He probably has quite enough problems with his current situation, so he doesn't need any help in finding new ones. Discover what these problems are, and offer him the best solution.

Why Do People Buy?

Each customer is different, so what might be considered a

good reason to buy for one person will not necessarily apply to another. They all have different needs and wants. If you concentrate on the wrong need you will probably lose the sale, no matter how good your product or service is. So, until you have unearthed the customer's specific needs, do not even attempt to sell to him.

You should be able to identify what your product or service does that satisfies your customers needs and how you can improve upon this, so as to satisfy even more of his needs in the future. Look out for potential prospects who have the specific problem that your product or service can remedy. The more detailed you are about what problems your product will solve, the more people will want to use it. Customers are looking for solutions to problems, and nothing else. They are only concerned about their current situation; they don't really care about you or your product. All they're interested in is their problems or needs and whether or not your product can remedy their situation.

When a customer is convinced that he will benefit from owning your product or service, he tends to worry less about the price. If you can convince him that he will benefit greatly from your product, he will want to purchase it, regardless of the price.

The customer must be convinced that he will benefit far more from owning your product than he would from keeping the money necessary to buy it. In other words, you are informing the customer that, if he parts with his money, the product or service you will supply him with in return will be of greater value to him. So, he must be completely satisfied that if he purchases your product or service, he will be far better off than if he bought from somebody else. As I've demonstrated earlier, testimonial letters can be very persuasive in this regard. So, you should seek to obtain as many as you can from your satisfied customers. You will find that this will make selling much easier. So, always include them in your sales literature.

Just because the customer has intimated that he is interested in the product or service that you are selling doesn't necessarily imply that you have successfully negotiated a sale. It is vitally important to convince him that he has made right decision by choosing your company. You must be able to satisfy him that he will benefit from a high level of dependability and a low level of uncertainty if he purchases from you; otherwise you could lose the sale.

Chapter 30

ESTABLISH YOUR INTEGRITY

Everyone has, at some time in their lives, made a bad buying decision. Because of this they are afraid of making the same mistake again. Therefore, you should be aware of this and do everything in our power to put your customer's mind at rest. Constantly assure him that he will not regret buying from you.

In all sales, everything you do or say either brings the sale closer or moves it further away. This is especially true in the case of the larger sale. So, always be on your guard to ensure that everything you do or say is reassuring to the customer.

The higher the level of trust the customer has in you and your product; the lower are his concerns and fears about buying from you. When his level of trust reaches a certain level, the chances are he will decide to buy.

Remember, customers not only want the product or service they purchase to be reliable and efficient, they also expect that the person they are buying from meets those requirements. So, before you even consider selling your product, you should first ensure that the customer is convinced about your integrity and dependability. This will help lower his fear and uncertainty; because if the customer still has some doubts, there is little likelihood that he will consider your offer. The customer will want to know that he can rely upon you and your product to fully satisfy his requirements; otherwise he will not even consider parting with his money.

If, for any reason, the customer is not entirely convinced about your integrity, it is highly unlikely that he will buy your product. He will simply search around for someone who he feels he can trust more. This is why it's so important to build up the level of trust between you and your customer.

Customer Relationships

Customers nowadays are looking to establish a relationship with the supplier of the goods prior to making the decision about whether to buy or not. The relationship between supplier and customer is of utmost importance when it comes to selling anything.

To be a successful salesperson, you must establish long-term relationships with your customers; and continue this relationship even further by being reliable, attentive and caring. All this, combined with an excellent after-sale service and support.

Leave each customer in no doubt that you want to build and maintain a long-term relationship with them. This can usually influence their buying decision in your favour.

Keep in regular contact with your customers and let them know how much you value them as customers and friends. Also, make them aware of how much you appreciate the fact that they continue to do business with you.

Never take your customers for granted, this is the one thing that's guaranteed to ruin any sales relationship. Remember, you're not the only person selling this product or service. The only way to keep ahead of the competition is to ensure that your customers are happy and well looked-after. Your job is to find customers; and once you have done this, try your utmost to hold onto them.

People prefer to do business with someone they like, but are extremely reluctant to buy from someone they don't like, regardless of whether or not their product is what they want or need. With this in mind, you should always regard your customers as friends and treat them in a manner that reflects this. You will find that your most valued customers are people you like; and more often than not, people that like you too.

How the customer perceives you will determine whether the sale proceeds or not. He must think positively about your product or service before he decides to buy it. In his eyes, the most attractive products are the ones being sold by the most reliable and trustworthy company.

If the customer believes you to be the most dependable person to do business with, he will even be willing to pay more for your product or service because he knows he can rely on you to deliver on your promises. This is an extremely advantageous position to be in, because it neutralises your competition. The customer feels so strongly about you and your product that none of your competitors can come between him and you. When you're viewed by your customer as someone who gives them what they need, they will look upon you as a friend and will want to buy from you.

In order to build a high level of trust between you and your customer, you should take time to familiarize yourself with his most specific needs. This type of thorough preparation is what separates the successful salesperson from the unsuccessful one; they leave absolutely nothing to chance. Neither should you! Always prepare thoroughly prior to dealing with customers. Never get caught off guard due to the fact that you have failed to acquaint yourself fully with the details of your customer. Never rely entirely on your memory. Keep a file on each customer; and prior to each contact, review your notes. It's details like these that can make all the difference with regard to how the customer views both you and your company.

Never Leave The Customer Feeling Manipulated

Customers need to feel that they have made their own minds up when it comes to buying a product or service. They don't like to think that they have been manipulated into making a buying decision. Instead, the customer must feel that you have helped him to obtain what he wants and needs. In his eyes you must be someone who is helping him; as opposed to someone who is selling to him. If he perceives you in this way, he will want to do further business with you. He will see you as a trustworthy advisor who can be relied upon to help customers come to the right decision and get what they need.

If your customer suspects that you are trying to coerce him into buying your product, he will immediately pull-out of the sale. You will have lost his trust. Losing the trust of your customer is the worst thing that can happen to a salesperson, so you must ensure you never do anything to jeopardize this most important factor.

Believe In Your Product

If you truly believe in what you're selling and are enthusiastic about it, the customer will pick up in this vibe. You should transfer your enthusiasm into your marketing materials, the results will truly amaze you. But, on the other hand, if you don't really believe in your product, people will sense it, and you won't get their business. If you believe you are selling the best product or service to the right customer for the right price, this is the ideal situation for all concerned. All parties are having their needs satisfied.

In order to enter into further transactions with your customer, it is essential that he is satisfied with the outcome of previous business dealings he has had with you. If he feels positive towards you, he will happily choose to do further business with your company. So, you must always ensure that you leave each customer feeling that he would be happy to continue doing business with you in the future.

Chapter 31

THE POWER OF PERSISTENCE

Remember, failure cannot live with persistence. Be positive about what you are about to embark upon and what you're going to achieve. As long as you have a positive mental attitude, you will ultimately have full control over your life. Your energy levels will increase and you will become far more inventive and accomplish greater things.

Start today by deciding exactly what it is that you want to do and achieve. Set your sights high. Aim for goals that both frighten and excite you; but make sure they're achievable and measurable. Take action today! Don't ask for anybody else's opinion. You are the best judge of what is best for you. Live your life according to your own timetable; not somebody else's.

There are no limits to what you can achieve, except those that you place on yourself.

Take the first step towards a happier, more productive life.

GOOD LUCK!